This book attempts t

is essential in reaching the potential that lies within all of us.

Society - (family, parents, persons, etc.) can easily stifle our creative abilities by instilling guilt in us for not conforming to all the so-called norms (rules) established by them.

A lot of humor too!

International Standard Book Number 0-9619152-1-8

First Printing; September 1993

Printed in the United States of America

Dedication

This book is dedicated to all former stinkers and who are thinkers and especially to those who still are in the stinker stage.

LB

Quotes

"This book is more revealing than Madonna's latest book."___ A Critic

TABLE OF CONTENTS

FROM STINKER TO THINKER

Introduction

A Fantasy Come True

In my speeches, I talk about my life being a fantasy come true. To many, I am sure, my life doesn't seem like such a big deal. However, knowing where I started and knowing where I ended, seems like a miracle to me.

If I had dreamed of being a public speaker as a youth growing up in Beaver Creek, and had the audacity to announce my intentions in public, I would have been told, "Oh, sure, you talk too much, Luther, we know that, but regular people don't get paid for talking. Only the preacher does. And not much either. We try to give him as little as possible. We give that offering three times a year, you know."

No one would have taken me seriously. I wouldn't have even taken myself seriously. That is why this second book has been so important to me. I know there are others in the world that are struggling with the same self-doubts about their abilities as I did. I know there are others that see the struggle as not being worth the effort. I know that there are those that are afraid of risks or are hindered by sensitivity and mis-direction in much the same manner that I was.

That is why I want to reach as many people as possible with the message that WE HAVE THE POWER WITHIN EACH OF US TO REACH OUR MIRACLE - OUR FANTASY. I want to help people save as much time as possible on their journey by sharing what I have learned. Whether you are eighteen years old, or eighty years young, your miracle can be reached. And if we can have a few smiles along the way, that is even better.

Motivational speakers will tell you that you should write down your goals and keep them secretly hidden somewhere. I didn't even think of writing those things down in my youth because they were absolutely too far fetched to be real. I thought, "What if I have to explain these far-fetched goals sometime because somebody found them?"

Now I know we have the power within us to reach our goals. How long does it take? Many of us die before "our miracle" has a chance to happen. That is a tragedy. A waste of life. I was forty-six years old when I began to realize my dream. I wasn't ready any earlier. I would like to help other people to be ready earlier so that they can enjoy it longer.

We are the center of the universe. Not in an egoistical sense of the word, but in the sense that we view everything and everyone else around us from our own particular standpoint. That is why it is so important to be the best we can be and to really know ourselves. As long as we know who we are and where we are going, we will be successful and happy.

All of us have moments when we are down. There is no denying that. We wonder if life is worth what we are going through at the time. But usually the negative thoughts pass as conditions improve or as we encounter other mountains we wish to climb. Sometimes, however, the negative thoughts linger when we start to search desperately for a definite meaning for our lives or when the mountains don't seem to be looming in our horizon anymore, or look too large to climb on our own.

It is at times like these that we need to realize and accept that the true meaning in life, and life's greatest joy, lies simply in the search. There are no single answers for any of us. The meaning is in the living, the sharing, the searching, and in the laughter. Our only responsibility in this life is to be the best we can be. No more. No less.

Like my friend Ole says, "I don't know vy people are so ankshus and so concerned and so vurried about life. It's so short. Besides, I came into this vurld naked. And no matter vot happens, I'm going to leave in a new suit."

We are much too anxious about life. It becomes obvious when occasionally, I ask an audience, "How many of you started a little task today and when you finished it, you stood back, examined it and said, 'perfect'." Often times, not a hand will go up. Then I ask, "How many of you have done anything, anything in your life, that when you finished it, you stood back and said, 'perfectly done'." Still usually not a hand raises. I then say, "Then lighten up. Just lighten up. If that's the case, lighten up and go for it and stumble and fall." Like my friend Ole says, 'Dey said it couldn't be done, but I tackled it vit a smile ...... and I couldn't do it.'

So what! The greatest achievements of

mankind were accomplished by stumbling and fumbling. In fact Thomas Edison, to invent the light bulb, went through a series of failures - 2,500 - until he invented the light bulb. He said, "You can't learn from success. It just doesn't stay with you. But I know 2,500 ways of not being able to invent the light bulb."

I like that. Once I understood that we can learn from our mistakes, my life changed for the better. When it finally soaked in that we are responsible for much of the course of our lives; that we are the masters of our souls; the captains of our fate; we will realize that we are responsible for our actions. It is a wonderful thing. We can't say "a committee did it". The buck can't be passed to anyone else. And that is a wonderful thing.

If anybody reads this book and gets some inspiration, a chuckle, a memory jogged, or a direction from it that makes their life better, I will have accomplished my goal.

All of us need to understand that there isn't a day that we'll feel perfect, but we can still move forward inspite of all these imperfections, to become better human beings.

I have a friend by the name of Harold Wenaas. He has a granddaughter, Amy, who, at sixteen, came down with multiple sclerosis so severely that she was confined to a wheelchair. But what an amazing attitude she has had! It has helped her through some of the darkest hours we as humans can encounter. Despite her disability, she strives to do and be everything she has always wanted to do and be while at the same time, making everyone around her, glad to have made her acquaintance.

What should Amy's story tell us? Forget about all of the sensitivity you may have felt in the past. Live! There are times to be sensitive to other people, but don't be self-sensitive -selfish. Some people get so bound up in "self" that they can't go out of their own home and associate with others -with life! Being bound physically or mentally are both tragedies. Most of us need to count our blessings and share them with others.

It always gives me a boost to go to the nursing home, if I am becoming too sensitive to other people's reactions to what I am doing. I leave the nursing home thankful that I am alive and well, but also knowing that there will be a time, sooner than I realize, that I will not be able to function the way that I can today. So my advice is to get out there and get a hold of life, as much as you can. Say "yes" to things you've said "no" to life for many years. Say "yes" to nearly all opportunities. The younger we are when we start saying "yes", the greater fulfillment we will have in our lives.

Do I ever say "no" to things? Well, if someone calls and says, "Is Luther Bjerke there? We'd like him to perform surgery on a patient, here at St. Lukes' Hospital." I'd probably say, "Sorry. I'm tied up today."

I do have my limits. One has to be very careful about being kind of arrogant too, you know.

Someone asked me the other day, "Luther,

what is the meaning of life?" I think it was meant to be a flippant question, but I responded anyway. I said, "Don't worry about the meaning of life. Don't search for the meaning. The meaning is in the living. You live and the meaning comes. Don't spend all of your time contemplating your navel and asking, 'What is truth?' There is no result to that. Just live. Don't say "no" to the opportunities that come along, if you think you can do the job even half-way worthwhile. Say 'yes', and if you screw up, that's okay. Someone will help you along the way. Unseen hands are guiding you.

CHAPTER ONE

Was I Stinker, or a Beginning Thinker?

At times, I will admit that growing up, there were those around me who would have called me a "stinker". Those unenlightened few who didn't understand the emerging spirit of a child - that natural curiosity that takes a child from being a soft lump of mindless clay - to being an adult with a unique personality and background.

But even in those days, as I emerged from my cocoon, I preferred to call myself a "reporter" instead of "stinker". I saw myself as a vessel that was open to be filled. I saw myself as a recorder of life's experiences -an observer that sampled life's fare and then shared impressions of it. But was I at times a stinker? Well, I'll admit to being a nuisance sometimes. And sometimes my questions were as rapid-fire as a howitzer. And admittedly, "tact" wasn't a word that came early to my young vocabulary.

The Harelipped Neighbor

Near our home, for example, there was a neighbor who had a severe cleft palate. Occasionally he would come over to visit and share our dinner with us. He was a nice man, but I couldn't quite get past his unusual appearance. One evening as we were all sitting around the table, (as my mother told the story later) I was mesmerized by how our neighbor compensated for his harelip as he slid food off his fork. I watched his mouth make special configurations to compensate for his impeded speech. My mother knew, as mothers often do, that I was eventually going to say something. She tried to distract me with the potatoes. It didn't work. She tried to draw me into the conversation, in order to break the spell that the harelipped neighbor had over me. It didn't work. She wanted to admonish me with: "don't say what you are going to say," but how could she say that without making matters worse?

Finally, my curiosity burst forth on my lips. "How come you have such a funny face?" I asked.

My mother said there was a deadly silence in the room and she felt the perspiration bead up on her nose.

"I guess that is just the way I am," our neighbor replied.

That was all I needed. I was ready for dessert.

Too Much of a Good Thing

One time, during my "stinker" stage, I was going with my mother, to visit another neighbor, Emma. None of us were wealthy in our community and Emma had even less than the rest of us, so as Mother and I were walking across the uneven prairie on the way to Emma's, she warned me, "If you are going to say anything to these people, be sure that it is something nice."

Mother's words echoed in my ears as the afternoon went on and I tried my best to fulfill her request. "Oh, these walls are so beautiful, Emma," I said. "The floors are so nice, Emma, and so is the door. This is the best bread I have ever had, Emma. This is a very nice table."

My intentions of overlooking our neighbor's poverty soon became obvious when Emma brought out a milk pitcher that was shaped like a corncob. It was cracked all the way down the front and it's entire lip was missing. But as she poured the milk through the v-crack in the front, I said, "This is the prettiest pitcher in the whole world, Emma."

My mother handled the situation well. She never again pointed out what I was supposed to overlook. She realized that once a seed was planted in the fertile mind of youth, it just had to grow and grow and grow whether it was a weed or a rose.

Get Along Little Cowboy

The power of suggestion took a strong hold on me in my youth. I remember a bronco we had one time. It was a white horse with an "LOU" branded on the side. In those days, the neighbors used to buy horses by the carload and then each of the neighbors would buy what we called "partials" - a couple of horses each. Usually the horses came from out west and were unbroken.

This particular horse, however, was broken and he was a very good cutting horse. We never used it as a cutting horse, though. He was for riding and for rounding up the cattle.

One day, someone told me that broncos were well trained and that no matter how fast you are riding, if you drop split reins, the horse will stop immediately. Of course I had to find out for myself.

As I remember it, the sun was setting in the West. The trail was dusty as this lone rider sauntered into the sunset on his trusty white bronco. Boy and horse, like a continuation of each other, not even a saddle between us, cutting a picture-perfect shadow against the sunset.

After heading out to the range at a distance that would allow the horse to lather well before reaching the barnyard, I headed to the barn from the North, at the absolute fastest gallop possible.

And dropped the reins.

My ride lasted longer than the horse's. He stopped a few yards back and I continued on. The darkness fell a little earlier for me that evening than it did for the neighbors.

The Stork's Stark Facts

I wasn't necessarily considered a normal child. I was, perhaps more wide open to life than other children my age. I was like an empty cup. More empty it seems, than the neighbor children were.

When I was eight or nine years old, my mother became pregnant. We children knew my mother was going to have a baby. We also knew a great deal about the reproduction processes of the cattle and the horses. I had seen the bull breed the cows. Somehow I didn't make a connection between the animals and my mother. In fact, I didn't even know that the baby was INSIDE her.

One day my cousin and I were walking together and he said to me, "Your mother's going to have a baby." (He was older than me and thought he knew everything.)

"Yup," I replied, kicking up dust as I walked and occasionally throwing a stone at nothing when I wasn't hitching my thumbs on the back pockets of my britches.

"What do you want?" he asked.

I said matter-of-factly, "It's going to be a boy."

"How do you know?" he asked.

"We ordered it," I said confidently. "And the doctor will bring it in his little black bag."

Immediately he told me what my mother and father had done to cause this to happen.

"No way!" I hollered at him, and ran all the way home.

It was one of the few conversations I did not report to my mother. I just stared at her belly, on occasion, just in case I had been misinformed.

Where do Polka Dots come From?

Sometimes, I was thought to be more gullible than I was thought to be a stinker. When I was in seventh grade, there was a store in Hatton called the Farmer's Mercantile Store. When I came into town, one of the things I liked to do was hold the door open for the ladies that were entering the Farmer's Mercantile Store. It wasn't for the tips, believe me. I opened the door repeatedly, and in all those years, I only got a nickel. No it wasn't for the money. It was for the praise. I admit it. Each time one of those nice ladies would praise me, I would swing that door wider and with more snap for the next one.

But I liked to hang around The Farmer's Mercantile Store for another reason too. I knew the guy that managed the grocery part of the store and I knew that I could make money for running errands. Every time I was in town, I'd ask, "Do you got any errands?"

One day, I was probably more of a pest than usual, and when I asked, "Do you got any errands?" the manager said to me, "Yes, Luther, why don't you run across the tracks to the West Side Grocery Store and get a #2 bag stretcher?"

So I went over to the West Side Grocery Store and found Mr. Thompson, the owner. "They sent me over from the Farmer's Store to get a #2 bag stretcher," I announced in an authoritative and business-like voice.

"Well," Mr. Thompson said, "You can go back and tell Alfred that we don't have a #2 bag stretcher, but we have a #1 bag stretcher."

So I went back to The Farmer's Mercantile and delivered the message.

"Hmmm," Alfred said, "That's too bad. We can't use a #1. But why don't you run over to the drugstore and get some polka dot RIT dye?"

So I went over to the drugstore and I told Sam Haakenson, "I'm running errands for the Farmer's Store and they want some polka dot RIT."

They had the RIT in one little area, so Sam looks through all the packages, scratches his head and says, "Well, I'll be. We're just out of polka dot RIT."

So I went back and I told Alfred that Sam didn't have any polka dot RIT at his store. He was fresh out.

I still haven't seen any polka dot RIT and I haven't had many calls to seek out a #2 bag stretcher, but I don't regret having run the errands. You see, I would rather be trusting, and perhaps a little naive, than to have been suspicious and a know-it-all.

By the way, how does one get polka dots on fabric?

Elsie, the Teacher, and Oh the Things I Learned!

There was a teacher by the name of Elsie Eide who stayed at our place when I was eight years old. She liked me most of the time. Kept me after school often. I think it was for the companionship, but my mind is a little fuzzy as to the real reason.

I had a couple of slip-ups in my relationship with Elsie, the school teacher, however. But I learned from more than the lessons she gave at school. For example, I learned that I should be more patient for surprises.

One day, Elsie's mother and her boyfriend came over to surprise her with a visit. They had traveled quite a distance for this surprise and we were all informed that their presence would not be made known until Elsie ventured down the steps from her upstair's room.

I went along with this to a certain point, but the waiting seemed to be getting awfully long. In my mind Elsie could have been better using this time to visit and have coffee than to be upstairs without knowledge of her loved ones' arrival.

Before anyone could stop me, I hollered up the stairs, "Miss Eide, your mother and boyfriend are down here to see you. You better come down now."

Just about the time everyone had forgiven

me for that episode, I learned another lesson. This lesson was of multiple importance. It had to do with honesty and discretion.

One very cold winter night, there was a knock at our door. When it was opened, there stood one of my teacher's boyfriends, Melvin. He had walked nine miles when his car stopped and wouldn't go any further. (We lived twelve miles from Hatton.) Melvin stood in his oxford shoes and dress coat and a shell of ice all about him.

When my brothers and sisters went to bed at our usual time of 10 o'clock, we left Miss Eide and her boyfriend to visit in the kitchen. Now it just so happened that my brother, Duane, and I shared a bedroom and this bedroom was located just above the kitchen. It also just so happened that there was a heat register under our bed and above the heads of the young couple.

Shortly after prayers, and shortly before falling asleep, I crawled over my brother Duane and crawled under the bed. Lying there on my belly, I could feel the warm air wash over my face and hear the private conversation below me. Perhaps I was overly-stimulated by the witnessing of young love, perhaps it was the enjoyment I was experiencing in being a part of their time together; but for some reason, I broke out in my own rendition of the popular song, "Too Much in Love to Say Goodnight". I sang it with feeling through the heat register to the couple below me.

As I finished crooning, I could hear Elsie coming up the stairs. She walked into our bedroom and started to talk to Duane. She scolded him for the provision of mood music through the heat register in the kitchen.

All the while I was still hiding under the bed.

Another lesson I learned through Elsie was how to use a bit of creative trickery to get what I wanted. Well, actually, it wasn't directly through Elsie that I learned this. It was through her boyfriend who came to see her from Valley City, where he was going to college.

This boyfriend had an old car and when it was time for him to go home after his visit, the car wouldn't start. My dad pulled him around the yard with the horses trying to get the car started. That didn't work, so he had to spend the night.

The next day, Dad was becoming desperate to send the young love interest on his way, so he crawled under the car with a torch to heat the oil pan, hoping that would be the trick for getting the car started. But that didn't work either.

The following day, Elsie's boyfriend got a call. He found out that the band he played with finally got a playing engagement, so he went out to the car and lo and behold, the car started and took right off.

Elsie married him.

A Rural Boy Learns A Rural Lesson in the City

I was in the army at Fort Huachuca Arizona. On one of our first weekend passes, three of us went up to Tucson. We went to a restaurant to have a nice steak dinner. When a salad was served with the meal, it took me by surprise. I had never had a tossed salad at home before. Being a true-blue Scandinavian, most of my food to this point had been white, with a cream sauce over it for color. My two friends, being familiar with the custom of salad, gladly took this foreign food away from me and consumed it.

While they were eating the salads, I used the time to glance at the decor around the room. There was a great big mural on the wall that caught my eye. It had hundreds of cattle and some men sitting around a camp fire in a desert setting with mountains in the background. Accompanying the mural was a sign that said, "Rocky Mountain Oyster Feed".

I pondered this for a moment, and then asked my friends, "How in the world can they have oysters in the mountains?"

That was when I learned about rocky mountain oysters. That was when the salad didn't look so bad. That was when I realized how I appreciated friends that didn't capitalize on naivete, but understood that each of our backgrounds is different, and that difference doesn't take away from the person. The only thing that takes away from the person is the lack of desire to learn.

Was I tattle tale? I prefer the word "reporter". Was I stinker? I prefer to think that it was more curiosity and a love of life, (although presenting me in a less than favorable light at times), that gave me the experience and courage to be a thinker as an adult.

CHAPTER TWO

The Emerging Years

I have two brothers and a sister and as we were growing up, we were taught that virtuous children were seen, but not heard. I sometimes think that I would have been better off if I had stayed in Mother's womb until I was twenty-one and then came out and got a job. Then I wouldn't have had to go through this trauma called childhood.

I grew up at a time when the squelching of self-esteem was much more severe than it is now. I have allowed my own children more freedom to be themselves. Their self-esteem seems to be very good. (In fact, they feel so good about themselves sometimes, that they have had boyfriends and girlfriends that were worthless). But things were different in my day. We didn't have television. We weren't able to travel as easily or get out as much to see things. When I grew up, we were confined to a small area. Even going to Grand Forks was a special full-day trip.

One of the few places we did get to go was church. Even as a child, I found humor in everything - even church. Sometimes I would be reading Bible verses in Sunday School and I'd notice a straight line that needed to be looked at in a humorous way. Pastor Njaa, the adults in Beaver Creek, and God (I was told) did not take kindly to smiling or laughing at the straight lines in the Bible. But deep inside, a little voice would pause at some of the lines written by the prophets and say, "Oh oh. Let's take a look at this."

Now I'm old enough to do this without being sacrilegious or ridiculous. But I think in my day, the attitude toward children stifled their growth and creativity. The teachers at school also carried on the attitude of the church where children were concerned. I remember a teacher saying, "Oh Gaylor is such a nice boy. He sits in the corner and doesn't say anything." I remember thinking," He's sick! What kind of human being is that? That's not natural. Somebody should help that boy."

Oliver Scramstad and the Life-long Lesson

One of the best lessons I ever learned didn't take place in a classroom, but did involve a teacher. It didn't take place within the few minutes that lessons often occur, either, but over a life time and thousand of miles.

The teacher's name was Oliver Scramstad and he was my first grade teacher. I saw him when I was in the first grade at school and then not again until about four years ago. He had gone away from the area after my first grade year and I didn't care to see him ever again.

Something happened that changed my mind.

One day, about four years ago, my friend Elroy Lindaas, a ham radio hobbyist, said to me, "I've got a message for you from Oliver Scramstad, Tucson, Arizona. He asked me to tell you 'hello'."

The growing years

Oliver Scramstad, Luther's first grade teacher 1936.
Picture taken in Tuscon, Arizona in 1985 on a visit to see him.

Pastor Njaa at 100 years old
Elmer Bjerke (father), son Mark Bjerke, Luther Bjerke.

Joanna & Luther

Leann married Richard Bowman. They have five children, Christopher, Melani, Heather, Jay, and Kipp.

Lucinda Bjerke

Lynette Bjerke

Mark married Deborah Rioeplle. They have three children, Gillian, Alexander, and Chelssa.

Marla married John Beuchner. They have three children, twins Matthew and Andrew, and Carly.

Elmer and Ellen Bjerke, Luther's parents

Varsity Bards - 1958

The farm...

1916

1958

1990

"You pass on the message to him that I enjoyed the greeting and greetings back to him." I thought that would be the end of the pleasantries and didn't give it any more thought.

Sometime later there was a message on the answering machine at home, "Luther, this is Oliver Scramstad, just saying 'hello'."

Here was a man I hadn't seen since I was six years old and now I am....a lot older. I never knew anything about what he was doing. On other occasions, there were other messages. "I just wanted to say 'hello' to you, Luther."

I was never there when he called, so I just kept getting these messages. The messages seemed a little sad and carried some strong emotions, so when I was speaking in Mesa, Arizona, I rented a car and called to let Oliver Scramstad know that I was coming to visit him.

When I got there, I found that this man was a paraplegic. He could hardly eat his food without using a great big spoon. He had a 24-hour-a-day nurse in his home in Tucson. He wasn't quite bedridden, but he knew that his condition would get worse until someday he would even have to have an automatic voice activator on his radio equipment because his muscles would stop working.

Oliver Scramstad told me that he had been following my career. He even had my first record album jacket on his wall.

As we visited, I asked him, "Do you remember when you kicked me out of school?"

"No! I did?" he said in amazement.

"Do you remember Levern Bjerke?" I asked.

"Yeah," he replied.

"Well, he tripped you as you walked by. I don't think he meant it but he was a big boy and his foot came out and you tripped over it and you kicked him out of school. He was in the second grade."

"Well, I kind of remember a little bit about that, but not very much. But I do remember when you came up to me and said, 'Kelly Ness is sleeping'."

I didn't remember that. Kelly had been up with the sheep all night again I suppose, and had fallen asleep in school. I guess I was just doing my usual reporting.

"I remember when you kicked me out of school as vividly as if it had happened yesterday," I told Oliver. "I saw Levern out of the south-view window about 300 yards down there, sitting on the snowbank after he had been kicked out of school and you said, 'Anybody else does that, they'll get the same treatment.' About that time, my foot was out in the aisle, and of course you stumbled over it. (I was just a little guy, six years old.) It was just a reflex action, no malice or anything and so I got kicked out of school."

"I can't remember that," Oliver said.

"I want you to know that my folks heard

about it before I even got home. My punishment was that they knew what happened and it was embarrassing."

"Oh, I didn't know that," he said, "But I do remember a lot of other things that you did.

I left his home that day after a nice, long visit. I would hear occasionally from him through the recordings on my answering machine and through my friend, Elroy. In the meantime I sent him some speaking tapes and albums.

Then one day as I was leaving the yard, I stopped at the mailbox to get the mail. There was a letter from Oliver Scramstad's nurse. "I enjoyed having you come and visit us. Oliver really enjoyed having you here. It was one of the high points of his life as I know it. He died and at his funeral, he requested that they play your album where you sing, "How Great Thou Art". Many times he played it when he was alone and every time he'd say, 'Nobody can sing it like Luther'. He thought so much of you. He followed everything that you did. Somehow or another you were extremely special in his life."

I could have hated this man for the rest of my life for kicking me out of first grade when there was no intent of maliciousness. Look what I would have missed if I had taken that attitude. But I don't want to ever walk down any street in the world, without holding my head high. I want to look anybody straight in the eye.

I know people who will avoid another

person when they walk down the street, especially in a small town. It is easier to avoid a person in the big city, but in a small town, it is much more obvious as to what is going on. What a tragedy. I know there are some things that can't be fixed and you have to let go. I think the Bible says it pretty well when it says that if you've done everything possible within your power to correct a situation, and it doesn't work, let it go.

Spare the Rod and Spoil the Child

I was lucky that my parents didn't follow closely, the prevailing self-esteem crushing attitude of the time. In fact, I can't remember anything negative that my parents did to me as a child. They disciplined, but I knew I deserved it when it happened.

One time I stayed at the neighbor's house after school when I wasn't supposed to, and my sister came over there and said, "Mom wants you to come home."

I came home, eventually, and my mother was standing in the yard with a switch in her hand. That was serious business to a young boy. I saw her look at me through tear-filled eyes, (hers, not mine) and said, "Go into the bedroom and take down your pants."

I did what I was told. (Realizing, of course, that if I had done what I was told in the first place, I would not have ended up in this situation.)

My mother came into the bedroom and said

the age-old cliche, "This is going to hurt me more than it does you."

I mumbled a comment as the switch was raised and brought down with the fury only God could instill in a parent who feels the responsibility of a wayward child, and it stopped just short of the trembling, never seen the sun, goose flesh, of my back-end.

"Now. Let this serve as a lesson to you," she said with as much relief as I felt.

No Use Crying Over Spilled Milk

Another time in my journey from being a stinker to becoming a thinker, I was supposed to help my father by watching the cows. He wasn't going to tie them up. He brought them into the barn one at a time and put them in their stalls. I don't remember why, but the cattle were sort of milling around on this particular day. My father was finishing milking the last cow and he asked me to watch the two full pails of milk setting on the barn floor (the total we got daily).

Somehow I got distracted and didn't do my job. The cows tipped the two pails of milk over. I looked at the river of milk seething through the straw and droppings on the cement floor, looked up and saw my father rise and grab the leather strap hanging on the hook in one fluid motion. It didn't take long for me to realize that some distance needed to be placed between me, the spilled milk, and my father.

There was only one drawback to my escape

plan. My legs were about a third of the length of my fathers. Before you can say the word, "mercy", my father was towering above me, strap in hand. But he didn't do anything. Not a thing. It was during this pause in action that I realized how I had let the family down. The milk was a source of income. I had shirked my responsibility. I was punished by my own thoughts.

The Beaver and the Exciting New Words

I didn't get by quite so easily the day I was hanging around with the guy that everybody called The Beaver. I was about five or six years old, wearing my favorite bib overalls and hanging around on the bridge by my home, when The Beaver joined me. We were dropping stones into the water on that lazy summer afternoon, just enjoying the sunshine and warm temperatures when all of a sudden, The Beaver said, "G#d/*#m dirty rotten s@#*^%b&*#h!"

I don't know why he said it. In fact, I didn't even know what it meant, but it had a certain pizazz. The rhythm was good and the enthusiasm that accompanied it was admirable. When I got home, I found my mother busy in the kitchen. I watched her for a little while, and putting my hands into the pockets of my bib overalls, I leaned against the doorjamb and said, "G#d/*#m dirty rotten s@#*^%b&*#h!"

It was then that she noticed I was in the room. Being the smart woman that she was, she didn't say, "What did you say? Because I would have surely repeated this new and wondrous thing I had just learned. No, instead she took me to the pump sink in the kitchen, took a bar of soap in her hand and said, "Come here, Luther."

So I went over to her.

"Stick your tongue out."

So I did and she put some soap on it. That was the end of that. I understood then that these were not the words you should be saying a lot. You didn't have to tell me more than once before I caught on. Fool me once - your fault. Fool me twice - my fault.

That was the last time I used those words, but it wasn't the last time that I learned some things from The Beaver of Beaver Creek. I flew down the Nyhus farm hill at 97 seven miles per hour in his Dad's '39 Ford with The Bull. I tipped a few toilets over with him, and he shared my interest in the new phenomenon I discovered at the age of thirteen -girls.

These are Pretty, I'll Take Two or Three or...

I had girlfriends at the age of thirteen. Of course it was all very platonic and when I tired of them or someone new took my interest, I left the "old" one behind as if they were socks with holes in them. It wasn't intended in a mean way. I would just quit. When it was over it was over. I never thought about if the girl thought it was over too.

I wasn't handsome, but I knew that I wanted the best looking girls to be my girlfriends. And it worked too. I don't know why. Apparently the girls weren't worried about finding the best looking boys.

This cycle continued for several years. I remember one time, when I was nineteen years old, I was kind of depressed. Things weren't going too good with the girl I was dating and my mother must have sensed this because she said, "Luther, do you always have to try to find the BEST looking girl?"

That was the only time that was ever said, but it must have struck me as profound because I remember it to this day. I accepted her comment as very wise, but it didn't change anything. Someone who was pleasant to look at was a necessity for me.

Stirrings of Talent

Besides being guided toward adulthood by my parents, learning new words, and discovering girls in my youth, I learned, also, that I liked to entertain people. I had put my sense of humor "on hold" during much of my teen years because I was so self-conscious that I was afraid I would make a fool of myself if I joked around or acted silly. But I loved to sing. My Mother was great at sitting at the piano and playing. Eventually she would say, "Luther, come here." And I would walk in concentric circles, around the house, sometimes outside the house, as I made my way to her at the piano. Mother would patiently wait and wait and eventually I would end up by her side.

She usually would pick an emotional song for me to sing. One of her favorites was, "Tell Mother I'll be There". It was a very sad song about a Mother who died and went to heaven. I sang that song when I was five years old in church and I remember singing the words, "Tell mother, I'll be there; In answer to her prayer; This message blessed Saviour to her bear; I'll soon be there, Mother," and looking at the ladies in the front row who were crying. It was the first time I realized that I could have an affect on people.

When I was sixteen years old, I went to a junior leadership camp in Jamestown where I sang "The Vienna Refrain". The next day I sang it on the radio and people came up to me later and told me that they cried when they listened to it.

We can go through life and find out only one person may say something real supportive about what we're doing, but it might be so sincere that it makes up for one hundred people who have said nothing.

When I was nineteen years old, the Farmer's Union hired me as a lifeguard. In my contract, it stated that I had to entertain the campers and visitors once a week by singing. Every week for five years during the summer, I was on the program for the final banquet. It's sort of "sick" when I think about it, but for many years I sang the same song, "Josephine", for the campers. "Oh there never was a girl I could love; Like I love my Josephine; She's a vamp, she's a scamp..."

Finally, one evening after another rousing rendition of "Josephine", the caretaker's wife came over to me and said, "Luther, I love your voice, but couldn't you pick another song?"

The next week at camp I came up with another song. Alma, the piano player played it beautifully. She could play anything, but in all those years, she was so kind-hearted that she never once suggested I change my direction. I don't remember what the new song was, now, because it wasn't important to me. Not like "Josephine" was.

CHAPTER THREE

The Discovery of Cars, Women and Other Fine Things

My First Car

I had a 38 Ford standard, two-door. My dad had it and then bought another car, so I got it. It didn't have brakes. At one time it had cable brakes, but the gravel roads chewed them up, so I had to slow down and put it in low gear as I approached a stop sign. (Since this car, I have never had to replace brakes because I learned to slow down before I get to a stop sign.)

Even though my 38 Ford was pretty limited in ability, I wouldn't let it stop me from doing things. I remember one winter we couldn't drive on the road because it was blocked toward both Hatton and Northwood. There was a girl in Northwood that I wanted to see, however. Motivation is the essence of that kind of activity, I guess. I drove the car to the barn and put chains on the wheels. Then I put a robe in the back seat and threw in a storm coat and two shovels because another guy was going to ride with me. We started driving when this little "clink" sounded in the transmission.

I should have known that my habit of throwing the car into reverse in order to stop without brakes, would eventually get me into trouble. On this particular day, some gears had broken off in the transmission. We couldn't keep driving with bits of metal in the transmission fluid, so we drove back into the barn, drained the transmission fluid, sifted out the bits of metal, and then poured the fluid back in. Off we went to Northwood.

Nothing should ever keep you from your goal. We shoveled our way there. When we got there, I only had two gears and neither of them was a reverse gear. I couldn't drive into a curb because I couldn't back up.

Used: Both Me and the Car

I had more learning experiences with cars. I eventually wanted a car with brakes. There was a 1940 Plymouth, beat up but it had two brakes and two doors. The car salesman wanted 350 dollars to-boot. Way too much, but I was a young man of nineteen and didn't quibble about the price. In fact, I didn't even ask for a guarantee. This honest used-car salesman offered me more information than I had requested, though. "The warranty on this beauty is 15% for thirty days for parts."

Boy was I impressed. I wasn't sure what it meant, but I didn't care. It had two brakes.

I drove the car for about a week when the engine mysteriously and without much fanfare went pfffft. It fell apart. So I took it back to the dealer and they fixed it up.

The bill was for $350.

I said to the honest used car salesman, Gilmore, "I thought it was under warranty."

"Yeah," Gilmore said. "But it was for 15% for 30 days."

"Well, what was wrong with the car?" I asked.

"It was just this one part, " Gilmore said, "But we knew you didn't want to leave the rest of it that way, so we overhauled it completely."

I asked, "How much was the part?"

"Seven dollars," Gilmore said. "I gave you 15% of the seven dollars."

It was the first time I had gone to the dry cleaners and I wasn't carrying a shirt.

Did I go through life being miserable about this? No. I tried to trade with him for twelve different cars after that to get even.

Here is how I react to life. I do not spit in the face of those who spit on me. I will turn the other cheek as the Bible advises. In fact, many years later, this man was standing on the street corner in Northwood. He was eighty-five years old at the time and I said to him, "Hi, Gilmore. How are you?"

He nodded in recognition.

"Say," I said, " I want to thank you for treating me so badly on the first car I bought."

"Oh?" he said.

Then I reminded him about what happened.

"Oh, I didn't know that," he said, in his same old, smooth salesman voice.

I didn't even remind him of the DeSoto I bought from him when I was a student at the University of North Dakota. It was a big, faded, four-door. It had 47,000 miles on it. My cousin, Earl (who was also one of my best friends) was a mechanic in the back of Gilmore's car dealership. He was watching from the shop as I was negotiating the price with Gilmore. I looked Gilmore straight in the eye and said, "Is 47,000 miles, the actual miles?"

"Well, I'm sure it is," Gilmore said as he looked me straight in the eye back.

Later, Earl told me that just that morning, Gilmore had ordered him to turn the odometer back from 93,000 miles.

But as I stood by that frail, old man on that street corner so many years later, I held no grudges. What good would that do? St. Peter was just around the corner, waiting to negotiate a deal on a used set of wings for Gilmore.

Finding Something Better than Cars

I loved to dance, go to movies and visit. I still do. I really liked girls (still do). But as a young man, I had no intention of getting serious about any one particular girl.

I liked many of them and they were my friends. The problem was, some of the girls were ready for a more serious relationship, and I wasn't. Until I was about the age of twenty-two the future for me was sort of a murky, distant darkness. I wasn't ready for a serious relationship or a serious job because I didn't have the education for one. What I wanted at that point in my life was to do what me and my friends usually did on the weekends. We would go to the tavern in Northwood or Aneta to have a beer. My friends would stay at the tavern until lunch hour (1:00 a.m.), but I would go to the dance by 9:00 and dance. There weren't many boys there at 9:00, but there were a lot of girls.

One girl, I remember, said to me, "You don't drink very much do you Luther?"

"No, I don't," I said in an innocent voice. And that part was true. I didn't need to get "primed up" to go dancing. I still don't. However, I didn't dare tell the girl that my intent at leaving the bar early, wasn't so much because I didn't want another beer. It was because I wanted to get to the dance while "the pickings" were good. Besides, when it wasn't crowded you could really swing. You could go all the way around and see the orchestra twenty times or so each song.

When did I grow up? I still haven't, perhaps. That's why I still ask questions like, "What happens if you cross LSD with Lutefisk?"

"You get a free trip to Norway."

I Almost Make a Big Mistake

I was in Wichita Kansas, when the girl that I had been dating back home came through there to see me on her way to Arizona. I took the job away from home to give myself some time to think about our relationship, and to decide if she was the girl for me.. When she came through, she told me that she wanted to get married and I almost went along with it, being the amiable fellow that I am. My sister, who was well aware of my reasons for moving to Wichita, was more wise. "Luther, you can't do that. Luther it is impossible for you to get married right now. You just came down here. You are working at Boeing. You are going back home in April."

I knew my sister was right. I figured if this was the relationship for me, it could wait a little until my life was settled and we got a few things worked out. The girl went on to Arizona and sent me a couple of letters. They were sort of threatening because she informed me, "If you don't come down here and marry me, there is a guy here that is kind of interested."

I almost succumbed to that, too. It would have been foolish, now when I have seen how happy two people who are married have to be, in order for it to work. I now know what a relationship has to be like, to be happy. But at that time, I didn't really know.

The Real Thing

A beautiful, wonderful woman named Joanna, (this isn't even a paid, political ad!) moved from Bottineau, North Dakota, with her four year old daughter, to live with her sister on a farm near Finley, North Dakota. Joanna was a widow. Her first husband died of a kidney disease.

Joanna worked at the county agent's office in Finley the summer I was working for the ASCS office in the same town. It was my job to check on noxious weeds on farmland, so I had to make several trips to Joanna's office to pick up brochures on noxious weeds. One never knew when new materials would come in that would help my one man crusade against these killers of fine crops, you know. It was suddenly my life's duty to protect the farmland in the Finley area, which required frequent visits to the county agent's office for "updates" and dates. You might say I was a bit obnoxious about noxious weeds.

Four months later, Joanna and I were married. I knew it was right. There was no hesitation. It just clicked. Isn't it funny how you know when it is right? And to think that I have weeds to thank for my happiness.

CHAPTER FOUR

The University of North Dakota

As a Student

The one thing I can unequivocally say about knowledge is that the more you learn, the more you realize that you don't know very much. No matter how much education we attain, we will never know very much.

My friend Ole went to the optometrist to have his eyes examined. The doctor told him to close one eye and read the chart at the other end of the room.

"I can't do dat," Ole said.

"Why not?" asked the optometrist.

"Vell, ven I close von eye, da udder von automatically shuts too! And ven I open da udder eye, da udder one pops open too. I yust can't do it!"

"Well, then cover your one eye with your hand," the optometrist offered.

Ole tried this and his coordination leaved something to be desired. He poked his finger in his eye. He got his finger caught in this nose.

In exasperation the optometrist took a paper bag and cut one hole in it, eye level and put it over Ole's head. "How's this?" he asked.

"Vell, dey aren't too bad, but I'd really radder hav vire rims like my cousin's got," Ole replied.

We don't know very much, but usually its enough to make a decent life if we do the best we can and take advantage of the opportunities and talents we are offered.

I really started to live when I became a University of North Dakota student. My self-esteem started to climb. I didn't have very much before that, not inside, not where it counts. My life started to open. I never knew that I could have this kind of life until I started at the university and associated with people who were real, living, lively, exciting and open.

I began to learn about the world around me. Prior to becoming a student, I was as naive about the differences in people around me as Ole and Sven were in their hometown supper club. Ole and Sven were sipping on a drink when a black man came in. Sven said to Ole, "Who's dat den?"

Ole said, "Dat's a black man."

Sven said, "Ver dey from?"

Ole said, "Dey're from Africa."

Sven said, "Ver's Africa?"

Ole said, "I don't know, but it can't be too far. He's in here every night."

I went from Beaver Creek into the army for two years. From the army, I went to the University of North Dakota as an older-than-average student. While a new student at the University, a friend of mine told me that the Varsity Bards, a campus men's chorus were having auditions and my friend wondered if I would like to come with him to audition? I didn't even answer him. I wouldn't have had the audacity to think that I was good enough to audition for something. You see, I was told by Reverend Njaa all of my life, that "You are no good, you are unworthy and you fall short."

I know he wasn't speaking to me particularly, but I had always felt I was the particular, especially since Reverend Njaa had been the minister there for thirty-six years and when he finally spoke English after years of giving sermons in Norwegian, I figured I'd better listen.

But the seed of singing had been planted. I started to think, "I want to do something with my voice. I have been singing all of my life in different ways and have enjoyed every minute of it."

I had been in every operetta Hatton High school had ever had. I had always loved music, so I began to look in the class schedule for an opportunity to enjoy music again and I found a listing for voice lessons. I had no idea how many students the class would include, but I was hoping that I could hide my voice in the class. Jim Fudge was the instructor and had at one time even sung with the Robert Shaw Chorale. I didn't know he was also the director of the Varsity Bards.

The first day of class, Mr. Fudge brought out the music that we were going to sing and explained that we would have different songs and have fun with them. The music he gave me was "Black, Black, Black is the Color of My True Love's Hair".

The Varsity Bards

At the end of the class, Jim said, "Luther, have you ever considered singing with the Varsity Bards?"

I mumbled some sort of a response that he must have recognized as an affirmation because he added, "Come over at 4:30."

In a small voice I answered, "O.K."

So I went over and sat in the auditorium and we practiced and practiced. Then during the midyear tour (right between the two semesters) we started our singing engagements. Just prior to starting, however, Jim Fudge asked me if I would consider being the narrator for our group. The narrator sounded like such a non-threatening title, I thought I could handle that. After all, he explained that the job only encompassed the announcement of certain things and the need to recite a couple of others.

We toured Northwood, Lakota and then Jamestown. I consider that first performance at Jamestown High School to be one of the turning points in my life. It was 9:00 in the morning and the students were waiting for us to come on the risers. We marched on and we were totally disorganized. I don't know why we came on wrong. Jim Fudge was not pleased. He looked through his thick glasses that made his eyes look even bigger than usual, and it was obvious that this was not a happy choir director.

We started singing anyway. The programs

were shorter for the high schools than they were for the evening concerts. I introduced the college songs, "Ohio University", "Yale", "North Dakota", and "Minnesota". But when I got to "Minnesota", I thought of "Ole and Lena", and for some reason, and with a Norwegian brogue, I told this story:

"I vas da hir'd man on Pappa Rasmussen's farm for many years. He hadda daughter named Lena and I vas so crazy about her. She'd help me vit da chores in da barn and I'd help her vit da chores in the kitchen. Ve'd stop and smooch venever ve could. I'd get rid of da dinner scraps just as quick as a vink 'cause pappa had a new garbage disposal. He kept a pig under da kitchen sink. Den ven Lena and I vanted to be alone, ve'd take a few svings 'round the garbage dump and the manure pile. Ve created quite a stink in the neighborhood, but ve vere alone, I'll tell you dat. Den on Monday mornings, ven ve'd vash our clothes togedder, I look in dat little vindow in front and see our duds entwined vit vun anudder, I'd get yust lumpy vit goosepimples. Especially ven her bloomers yumped up and waved at me.

On Saturday night, Lena and I were gonna go out and do da chores. Ve vere gonna go out and milk Yenivive, the brown and vite geurnsey cow. I sat on von side and Lena on da udder. Da udder side. Ya, dere's two der too. Den ve started to sqveeze our hands vould touch and I'd get yust lumpy vit goosepimples. Oh Lena had strong hands. Ven She'd sqveeze, she used to put dents in da bottom of da pail.

I vas sitting on my side milking and tinking, dis vould be a good time to slip da engagement ring on her finger. At least, I tought, it vas her finger. But for twenty minutes dat Saturday night, I vas engaged to Yenivive, da brown and vite guernsey cow.

It brought the house down. I couldn't believe that high school students would have been affected by this story. I looked back at the Bards and they were nearly falling off the risers. I sneaked a look over to Jim Fudge and his eyes were still large through his glasses, but his body was moving in a chuckle beneath his suit.

We needed to lighten up. From then on, when Jim introduced me , he introduced me as the "Wild Norwegian". He never thought I was wild. It was a sarcasm sort of like telling someone that they have "bold humility".

Stepping Down as Associate Dean at U.N.D.

For many years I worked at the University of North Dakota as the Associate Dean. Because I was so visible, many people thought I was the President of the University. My job was in public relations. I spoke at many graduations, recruited students, spoke to incoming Freshman and their families, worked as an advisor to students, and developed a public relations program at the University. It was a wonderful job and I loved it. Leaving was one of the most difficult decisions of my entire life. It was also one of the best.

Leaving the University came about in a somewhat strange way. Like so many other things in life, it seemed as if I was being guided by a higher power. It involved a decision that caused me some pain, but also caused me to grow spiritually.

Over the years I was employed as an Associate Dean, I spent time talking to the president, Tom Clifford. Every time, we visited, I'd leave his office feeling like I was in the clouds. It was so wonderful. He would build me up and give me incredible verbal encouragements about my work at the University. He told me to come up with my own title. I was an associate dean which was pretty good and I loved what I was doing. I couldn't imagine sitting at a desk somewhere, not being with people and I had the only job on campus that required being out with people.

"You should have been there," I'd tell my wife, Joanna, after a visit with the president.

But in actuality, Tom Clifford and I were playing games with each other, and admittedly enjoying it.

These games went on for a couple of years. One day after coming out of Clifford's office, I visited in the hall with a friend of mine, Vice President of Finance, Jerry Skogley. I related to Jerry some of the things that Tom had promised me and Jerry said, "Did you get it in writing?"

"What do you mean by that?" I asked.

"Nothing," Jerry replied. "Just asking."

A while later, Jerry and I were on a fishing trip together and I confided in Jerry that Tom Clifford and I had not come to a concrete agreement yet, as to my duties, title, and responsibilities.

"Well, he likes to play games with you," Jerry said.

I thought about what he said, and I knew he was right.

My contract was issued in April and became active on July 1. June 1 came around and I still hadn't signed and returned it. It was then that the "playing games" seemed like it was becoming closer to "side-stepping the truth".

When Wednesday, July 1, rolled around, as usual, I was in charge of registering students at Gamble Hall. My assistant, Bill McLain and I worked with fifty students a day. In the mornings I would address everyone and make some silly comments about the locations of the restrooms and how they need to go in the "in" door and out the "out" door and other rules of etiquette necessary for orderly restroom visits and other non-essential, light discourse. Then the professors advised the students on different topics.

At noon, I'd give a talk to all the students and parents at Wilkerson Hall for their noon meal. I was the focal point. They didn't meet the president. They met me.

But on July 1, after a regular registration day, I went home and announced to my wife, out of a clear, blue sky, "I am going to leave the university."

This was major stuff. I was the Associate Dean. My wife didn't have a job away from home. We had five children. This announcement represented a major life change for us.

My wife said, "It is up to you what you want to do."

The next day back at work, I went to talk to Jack Robertson who shared an office with me. "I'm leaving the University," I said.

"You are?" he said, eyes wide. "Close the door."

I closed the door. "What are you saying?" he asked incredulously.

"I really think that I have got to leave. I can't explain it. I've had it up to here," I said touching a high point at my neck. "I've reached a point that the balloon is exploding," I said in a rush of words.

"Wait until Friday," he said.

"O.K." I said, not sure why he wanted me to wait for Friday, but since I had no other immediate plans, I agreed.

On Thursday, I continued with registration as if nothing had changed. Jack Robertson came over to Wilkerson Hall and sat through the noon luncheon where I addressed yet another group of parents and students. He smiled. He laughed. He thought I was over my discomfort with my job because I was happy. Apparently he did not realize how important it is to me to make the best of the moment, no matter what the situation.

The next morning, I went back to Twamley Hall and I called Jack. "It's Friday," I said.

"You're leaving?" he said with surprise.

"Of course," I said. "You asked me to wait until Friday. It's Friday and I'm leaving."

"Just a minute," Jack said. "I'm going to talk to the president."

"If I don't hear from you by 10:00, I'm leaving," I said.

In the meantime, I had told my assistant about the situation so that he could take over when I left.

The clock ticked away and when the second hand on the clock was just hitting 10:00, the telephone rang.

It was Jack. "Luther, are you really leaving?"

"Yes," I said and turned to Bill, my assistant, "It's all yours."

There was no one home when I got home and I went into the bedroom and immediately laid down on the bed. I took off my shoes. (You are always supposed to do that, you know.) And I remember thinking, "What have I done? What have I done?"

I hadn't been home more than half an hour

when Bill, my assistant, called. He said, "I thought maybe you'd need a lift. Guess who came over to check to see if you really meant it about leaving? The University Busybody."

So word had spread fast. The University Busybody always wanted to have the first scoop. Somehow it made it all feel very official. I had been at the university for fifteen years. This was going to be a major change in my life.

Hatton had their big celebration the day after I resigned at the university. The Bicentennial celebration was going on and I was the emcee for the variety show. I had to go to the rehearsal the night of the resignation. No one knew that entire weekend about the major change that had just taken place in my life. I performed well that Saturday night. That told me something. If I could perform under that kind of strain and could still please people, I must have a real inner desire to do something in entertainment. It was a fleeting thought. I had much pain and other thinking to get through before I could pursue that idea further.

During one of those first days after the Bicentennial, Joanna and I sat over coffee together, just the two of us, and I thought, "Say it! Just say it!"

But she didn't say anything. If she had even said, "Do you think that you made the right choice?" I would have died. I would have just fallen apart. It was a painful reminder of how fragile we human beings are and why we aren't always willing to take risks.

Perhaps I didn't quite understand at the time that I had begun a quest to fulfill an unnamed need. I was so vulnerable that I wouldn't even go to a shopping mall because I was afraid I would see someone I knew and they would say something to me and it would bring on tears. Even my five year old daughter's request for a new bicycle was difficult to deal with. She had no idea what was going on in our lives or she wouldn't have made the request. All she knew was that Daddy was spending a lot more time at home now than ever before, so she offered to be my secretary and answer my telephone.

CHAPTER FIVE

BECOMING A PROFESSIONAL SPEAKER

The Beginning

After fifteen years as an Associate Dean, I began selling insurance. I sold insurance for two months. At that time, nothing was certainly happening as far as speaking was concerned. I discovered, during this interim, that patience is another virtue we need to understand. Besides being patient ourselves, we need to have people around us that are also patient.

I started selling life insurance to seniors in college, after I left the University. It was strictly life insurance and I hated it! I had left a $25,000 a year job for a $400 a month job and was beginning to question my own sanity. But strangely, when I was making only $400 a month, we had the first Christmas we paid for everything and had all the presents we wanted. Now tell me where THAT came from? It was like the Biblical story of the loaves and the fishes. It is a mystery to us still.

Even though we were making ends meet, I was in a dark, confused, "down" place in my thinking. It is true that life is an activity of the mind as well as a physical and spiritual activity. Perhaps an over-active sensitivity to everything around me made this time a little more difficult than it would have had to have been.

During this time, I was at a convention of the Conklin Corporation and got to know the chairman of the board, Bob Conklin. I didn't know him well on a personal basis, but during this dark period of my life, I decided to call him.

"Bob, I don't know what I am going to do," I told him during the course of the conversation. I've been offered all kinds of jobs, but I've been turning them down because it isn't the kind of work I want to do. I know you don't know me all that well, but I am really in a dilemma here. I have to decide if I should continue with the thought that I could be a public speaker, or if I should stay with selling insurance."

He didn't even hesitate. "Luther, forget the insurance. You can do much better in the speaking circuit than you will ever do in insurance."

I hadn't thought he really knew me, but he did. He left me with the thought that there shouldn't be any question in my mind that I should be a public speaker.

My conversation with Bill Conklin didn't remedy all of the problems, however. The dark days were still there, and one night after tossing and turning in my bed until nearly midnight, I started talking to God. "You know, I have heard all of these things, God about how people talk to you and how they receive some sort of response about their goals in life or their mission in life or some sort of guidance. Well, I really need help."

I continued this conversation with God until I fell asleep.

At about three o'clock in the morning, I woke up. I heard a voice. It was more of a sound, really, a sense of communication -a thought. Well, actually, more of an understanding. The understanding was, "Luther, go for the speaking. You've got what it takes. Go for it and don't look back. And when the doubts come, ignore them. Go for it like it's the only thing in the world."

I woke up and looked at Joanna. She was sound asleep. I got up, got a drink of water, and walked into the family room. I was just absolutely walking in the clouds. The answer had been there all along, but I had missed it. I had to search for it and plug my search into God. From that day I never looked back.

In January of the year I left the University of North Dakota, my life as a professional speaker started. I got a booking through Goose Johnson. He was the park's superintendent in Fargo. We met when he used to be in the extension office at the university many years ago.

"C'mon Luther," he said, "We want you to speak at a parks and recreation convention."

The convention was for thirteen states. This would be the moment of truth. Everything in my future would be determined by this speaking engagement. I wasn't really thinking about the pressure at the time. It would have been too much to handle. I just went out there and spoke.

Luther and 'Ole' big hit on Midwest lefse circuit

BY JIM BACCUS
Staff Writer

The Wild Norwegian, primped and duded up for the occasion, was in Fargo the other night, visiting with Farm Bureau members holding a convention.

Right behind him — in fact, stepping out of the Norwegian's skin for a comment now and then — was Luther Bjerke of Grand Forks, N.D. Luther may be the hottest after-dinner property and all-purpose banquet attraction in the Upper Midwest right now.

Luther (and the nameless Norwegian) were exactly what the Farm Bureau annual banquet committee needed. The convention delegates and their spouses had had a tough day of business. When Luther said his friend Ole had carpeted his bathroom and if the crops were good enough, he would run a sidewalk out to it, the audience belonged to Luther (and Ole) for the rest of the evening.

Many in the audience have roots in the Scandinavian peninsula and didn't need translation when Luther said that his name (Bjerke) meant "Birch place or area," from the little Norway community of Bjortomt.

When Luther's grandfather, Ole Erickson, came to the northwest, there were a lot of Ericksons around. Wanting some roots with the old homeland, Ole took another name.

Luther doesn't often spare either Ole or Lena, his neighbors in Beaver Creek Township, 12 miles west of Hatton, in Steele County. "A man asked me if I knew how to save a Norwegian from drowning," Luther said. I said, "No," and he said, "Good!." He added that up around Beaver "Crick" they bury Norwegians with their heads out of the ground because they last longer than tombstones.

Luther also kids himself. "I made an appearance in Memphis, Tennessee the other week," he said. "All evening, I was Mr. B-Jerk." Luther's accent is as thick as peanut butter.

Luther is in demand along the hard roll circuit and the Chicken- a-la-King civic luncheon world because there are really two Bjerkes.

There's the Wild Norwegian in his Aaron Slick costume with high-water pants, who can spin off dozens of ethnic jokes about Ole and Lena, sing parodies and involve audiences.

And there's Luther Bjerke who, facing audiences bedeviled by problems, encourages Americans to be proud but not too serious, to think kindly of each other and to smile.

"We need a sense of humor now," he says. "A sense of humor is seeing things as they really are. In our reactions to circumstances in which we find ourselves we automatically choose an attitude. And that attitude determines the way we think. Take time for laughter. Remember the song: "You've got to stop and smell the lutefisk."

The Bjerke combination of a motivational-inspirational speaker and a comic who can convulse any type of audience is irresistible to convention chairmen. Luther answers his own phones, arranges his own contracts and as a result is as busy as he wants to be. Right now he has booked dates into 1979.

Luther has faked out audiences in his own neighborhood as a Minister of Agriculture from Norway, as a director of the Norwegian Space Agency, as General Omar Norstad and as an aide to the King of Norway.

"I've fooled my own friends because they just didn't take a real close look at the platform guest," he said. "When they realize the crowd is being conned, it adds to the humor of the situation.

"I married Joanna Rosenau of Gardena, N.D., in Bottineau County," Luther says. "That was really a mixed marriage. My wife comes from a German family."

The Bjerkes have five children. "Ole likes to say they were conceived by every known method of birth control," Luther says. They include Mrs. Leann Bowman, Mark, who is observing his 18th birthday; Marla, 16; Lynette, 11; and Lucinda, 7.

It was a bold step for Luther, who is 47, to leave the faculty of the University of North Dakota after 15 years, to become a show business professional.

"My wife was uncertain about the move at first," he says. "Later I realized it was only because she thought I would be away from home a good deal. Actually, I have more time with my family now."

Luther was graduated from UND in 1959 with a master's degree in guidance and counseling.

After a stint with the American Red Cross, where he became the service's youngest field director, he returned to UND as an assistant dean and later an associate dean of the University College —generally serving freshmen.

"I was in a safe womb, a kind of warm cocoon at UND," Bjerke recalls. "But it was hard for me to encourage others to grasp life and live it to the full, and not do it myself. It was always my impossible dream, anyway, to entertain others. I knew that humor had helped me; I knew it could help others."

Naturally, Luther drew on his own roots for a good supply of self-deprecating humor, the kind that made his own family, his teachers and fellow pupils laugh.

There really is a Beaver Creek Township; the first settlers named it Norway Township

Permission from Fargo Forum

Fan Letter Comments

Our Tenth Anniversary was a success even though the weather was doubtful. This success belongs a great deal to people like yourself who took an active part in our program. We truly appreciated your presentation during the dinner meeting. I admire the special talent you have to speak in public, and am so pleased you were able to tie the dinner meeting all together to make it a big success.

In addition to sending along the enclosed check for your fee for speaking at our Suppliers Seminar on May 11, I want to personally thank you for the outstanding job you did. There's no denying that you were certainly the "hit of the evening," and your talk was the perfect finale of a most successful seminar.

We have been deluged with requests for your address and hope that you won't mind that we are complying with these requests. I'm sure you will find yourself even more in demand for speaking engagements.

What a humorous, inspirational message you have!

Perhaps you didn't realize it; you had a little bit of an antagonistic crowd initially. Many people remembered the "fiasco" we had at our Annual Meeting last year, and I think, were "daring" you to be funny.

I have never had so many complaints about a speaker before! Most will come up and say "why didn't he speak longer?", or some have said "I could have listened to him all day." I suspect some would not consider this a complaint, since most comments about speakers tend to be the reverse.

I wish to take this opportunity to thank you for a super job at the conference. Your humorous remarks really put a cap on the conference. I have had several people ask about the availability of your services, and I do believe you will get some additional engagements by virtue of this national exposure in our organization which uses many speakers.

Your outlook on life is very interesting and praticle. If everyone had your prospective, this country would be better off.

You were the highlight! Absolutely and unequivically the highlight! Thank you so much for the fantastic message you left with the members of the Savings League of Minnesota when you spoke at the Raddison "Springs" Hotel. The audience reaction was fantastic. I watched them and listened to them laugh and roar and practically fall of their chair one moment and the next moment they sat in absolute silence. If ever one held a group in the palm of his hand for thirty minutes, you did. The convention has now been over for two weeks, and in those past two weeks I have heard many, many comments and many chuckles relating to that evening when you so thoroughly entertained them.

"From Trash To Cash"

Barn built in 1910

Restored in 1980

1947 A - International Harvester

Restored in 1982

1947 John Deere

Restored in 1991

Continued

1917 Dodge Bros.

Restored in 1986-89

1934 Truck

Restored in 1992

1958 Honeymoon car

It had gone fairly well, I thought to myself as we drove home. Then quietly, from the seat beside me, my wife said, "It's going to be alright." That's all she said. It's all I needed her to say.

After that, things really started to move and the rest is just a fantasy. All of my bookings were through word of mouth. I didn't have an agent. Unbelievable. I didn't leave the university for financial reasons, but that too was enhanced. I discovered what I really liked to do and I was doing it.

Through speaking engagements I have had the opportunity to meet many people from around the world. One of those people was Lawrence Welk, the famous maestro from North Dakota. Mr. Welk invited me to be on his national television program, but it didn't work out. The letter he sent me is amongst some of my most treasured memorabilia. In it he says, "Your timing and delivery are fantastic. You are another Bob Hope." Of course those words ended up in my brochure. It's hard to pass up publicity like that!

Perhaps even sweeter praise to my ears, however, were the words my son spoke to a friend of his. "My dad sacrificed a lot for his family by staying home. He could have gone on to New York or Hollywood."

Then, a few years ago my son turned to me and said, "Dad, I understand that you are on Chicago's list of top speakers in the nation."

I don't know about the speaking list in Chicago. I don't know about the ability or even the desire to go to Hollywood or New York. But I do know about how lucky I am to be doing what I love to do without having had to sacrifice my family life.

I could stop working right now and feel that I have had a full and wonderful life.

Coming to an Understanding

Fourteen years after I left the University, I saw Tom Clifford at an alumni banquet. He was standing by himself and as I came up to him, he said, "How are you doing, Luther?"

"Really terrible," I said to him, "It's really sad."

His jaw dropped. This was very unusual because he always smiled.

I couldn't keep a straight face anymore. "It has been pretty wonderful," I told him.

He quickly said, "I knew that. I knew that. I've been following you." Then he added, "Luther I could have gone after you when you left, but it wouldn't have been fair to you."

I began to think to myself, "Oh, Oh. Here comes this game stuff again."

Tom continued, "You had outgrown the university, hadn't you? In fact, you had outgrown it a couple of years before you left."

I thought about what he had said and it was true. The parents and the students I dealt with at the university are still very close to me, but my life had to go on. The possibilities for lives can stop where you resign yourself to them whether it's for money or seeming obligations. At the time I was at the university, I thought I could stay there. I had a family to support and there was security if I stayed. "Was that the end of life?" I thought to myself when the security of the job nearly kept me at the university. But the realization also hit me that if this was my last opportunity and I was staying in it, then that meant that I was that much closer to death. I didn't want to reach the end of my life and find that I hadn't lived. Is life a matter of existing? Accepting what other people offer you? Or do you take a big bite yourself and make things happen?

You can't blame everybody else for your life. I've spent my share of time in the past, not taking total responsibility. "The committee did it. It is up to the committee." Was a pretty easy cop-out. The university was this womb-like existence. This womb handed out a paycheck like it was an umbilical cord. I didn't want to go through life without being able to reach out and live. I didn't want to just walk around with my umbilical cord in my hand just trying to find a place to plug it in. You have to let go. Cut the cord. Now, in retrospect, I never really lived until I took responsibility for my life - total responsibility with the help from others that is always there. Without that breaking free, I was not able, to say, " I am responsible."

I have more problems now than I ever

have. But they are mine and I can work them out with God's help. There is a power greater than us that will enter our lives if we'll let it. Electricity is like a spiritual power of God. If you want this power, you can't wait for someone else to plug it in for you. You have to reach out and plug it in so there is a direct connection to this great power, this omnipotence. Then you can go forward.

I see God and myself as co-creators. It is like that story of the farmer who bought this piece of land and it was nothing. Absolutely nothing. It was weeds and rocks. So he worked and worked and he developed it and he had a fine crop when the minister came over. The minister said, "Ole, look what you and God have done."

Ole replied, "Ya, but you should've seen it when God had it by himself."

Last February, I went to the Imperial Palace in Las Vegas for another alumni reunion. It was "Thank You, Tom" year because Tom Clifford was retiring at the end of the year. At the alumni banquet, Tom was standing by the hors d' oeuvre table all by himself. I walked over to him and said, "I think it's time that I thank you. This is 'Thank You Tom' year, so I'm going to thank you," and I shook his hand, "for what you have done for the university and for how things turned out between us." Then I added, "We were both sure playing games, weren't we?"

"Yes, we were," he said, smiling.

Then I reminded him of his comment a few years before about me having outgrown the

university - that it was too confining for me.
Then he said, "Talent plays a big role in that."

What a beautiful thing for him to say. At that moment in Las Vegas, all of the loose ends were tied up. Tom and I had closed the book. Why was he standing by himself at that moment in Las Vegas so that we had a chance to talk? I don't know. Never underestimate the possibilities of any situation.

I learned many things from this career change that I made at the age of forty-six. I learned that you have to do in life what you like to do. If you like it, you'll do it better than the average person. There will be good days and bad days in anything. If we can only learn in life that the way we do things might be different than someone else, but it is just as important that we do it our way.

Why did I have to be so old to learn these things? I don't care, as long as I learned them. Age is but a blink of an eye anyway. What is the difference if you are forty or fifty of sixty. Do things because you feel like doing them. I know society says the opposite. Society wants you to follow a certain path.

I had a dear friend who was a colleague at the university. He always gathered material to use in his speech writing. He shared material with me. I was in awe of him when he spoke and he was in awe of me because I LIKED to speak. He had a set of rules for his life. He was very conservative. When I left the university, this friend said to me, "You can't leave. I'd hate to see you on a street corner selling pencils."

Four years later, as I am going through a box of things I had had at my office at U.N.D., I came across a quote my friend had given me, from his collection of speaking materials. The quote was: "There is no one more stupid underneath the sun than one who would leave a job without having another one clearly in sight." I went against that absolutely. No wonder he was concerned. He didn't believe in the "risk".

I, on the other hand, did. I think of it often when I am lounging in the bathtub, practicing my speech before a performance. I think of the advantages of my work and how it has made me more sensitive to the people around me. I call myself an observer, but isn't that what everybody is? I observe and report. It has been an important part of my metamorphosis from thinker to stinker.

Sometimes human beings have difficulty bridging the communications barrier. My friend was worried I would be out of work. I was worried that I would not be working at something I loved. I was willing to take a risk of losing a secure job for finding a job that I loved. We did not understand where each other were coming from. We were not unlike the two friends, Ole and Sven.

Ole was sitting on a fence when Sven went by with a load of manure. Ole asked, "Where are you going, Sven?"

Sven said, "I'm going to put manure on my strawberries."

Ole said, "Don't you think sugar and cream would be better?"

But is it REALLY Work?

I can't describe my life to anybody. Maybe it's no big deal to other people, but it is to me. It is special. We were brought up to think that work has to be physical. There are people who think that I haven't worked a day in my life. I go right along with that. I say, "I haven't worked a day in my life."

Then I've gone too far and people say, "Well...."

What they are really trying to say is, "Luther, you never really worked very hard, did you?"

I try not be defensive because over the years, I have come to understand that small communities sometimes have the peculiarity of interpreting enthusiasm as bragging. Let me relate a true story that defends this theory.

One day I was visiting with a neighbor. "I see you have a new John Deere four-wheel drive."

The neighbor said, "Oh, gosh yes."

"It's a nice one," I replied.

"You know, Luther," the man replied, "I can cultivate many more acres a day with this new tractor than I could with my old one."

"That is so wonderful that you can do all of that," I commented, nodding my head in wonder.

"What are you doing these days, Luther?" the neighbor asked.

"I have just been in San Francisco at a beautiful hotel as a guest of the Manufactured Housing Association. They gave me a suite of rooms in this ornate hotel, with a fireplace, French doors and pictures with gilt frames. Each morning I could look out from the balcony over the city of San Francisco."

"Brag, brag, brag," was his response.

So the next time someone asked me what I had been doing, I said, "Nothing."

I have since changed my mind. It honestly hurt for a while. Enthusiasm as bragging? It was alright that he could say what he's done, but my kind of work was so foreign to him that he thought I was bragging.

That is one of the reasons I encouraged my children to leave their home community for a while after they grew up. I would encourage any child of any community to leave for a while after they are adults. Don't allow these things to happen to you that you have to conform to everybody and squelch your enthusiasm. If I hadn't, I may not have found the joy of doing what I love to do.

CHAPTER SIX

Mother and Father: Loving and Loved

Mother

Throughout my life I have tried to look at things in a positive way. It isn't always easy, especially when facing the death of someone precious to me. However, even death of a loved one sometimes has a subtle way of testing our strengths, and if finding us worthy of the test, leaves us stronger and richer in character.

Such a test came when my dear mother became very ill with amyotrophic lateral sclerosis (sometimes called Lou Gehrig's disease or ALS). She had been weakening for some time, but the doctors had been hesitant in giving her the final diagnosis since it is a devastating and terminal disease. The rehabilitation doctor also told us that when our mother came to the point of dying, we may have to make a decision about whether or not we would want her kept alive through artificial means.

In the meantime, we tried to keep her as comfortable as possible. She was a wonderful mother and deserved to experience the love and caring she had shown us. Her comfort was seen to at the nursing home in Hatton. We visited her often and one Memorial Day, death came to test our strength.

My family had spent the day at Golden

Lake. It was raining that day, sort of misty and cool; a day of thoughtful reflection. We had spent a leisurely morning and when afternoon arrived, Joanna and I told our children that we were going to run in to see my folks and that we would be back to pack up and drive back to Grand Forks.

When I walked into Mother's room and saw her lying on her bed, I knew that she would be leaving us soon. She whispered, "Hi" and scribbled a note with a pencil on her ever-ready pad of paper. The note said, "A magician will be entertaining in the chapel at three o'clock." I still have that note to this day.

Death was near. Perhaps it would seem easier to have run out of the room and leave without the tortuous good-byes, but I knew in my heart that I would face it. I also knew that out of the pain would come some good.

I went down to the nurse's station and asked, "What are we supposed to do when someone is dying?"

"Why?" the nurse asked.

"My mother is dying," I replied.

"No, no. She's not dying," the nurse responded.

But I knew she was dying. I was pleased that the nurses didn't know that she was dying. I wanted my mother to pass away with those who loved her most around her. I did not want strangers prolonging her misery. I had really known the true answer of what to do when I talked to the nurse. I just wanted to share the burden of what we were about to face, without bringing pain any sooner than need be to my wife and my father.

I went back into my mother's room and sat at the end of her bed. She whispered, "Happy birthday, Luther."

It occurred to me that my birthday wasn't for another ten days. It was then that I realized that my mother and I shared a secret much as we had done so often in the past. We shared the knowledge that she was dying.

I went around to the side of her bed, knowing that she was saying "good-bye" to me. I took her hand and told her how much I loved her. I hadn't told her that before. Tears were running down my cheeks in torrents. The fact that her eyes were dry struck me as odd. If I had told her that I loved her in the past, she would have gushed rivers of tears because she was a very emotional person. I realized, perhaps because of her dry eyes, that she had accepted death and was facing into it with the same courage and understanding she had displayed all of her life.

I stood by her bed for a time, following the urge to thank her for everything she had done for me as my mother. I told her how proud I was to be her son and how much I loved and respected her. As I poured my heart out to her, she slipped into a coma, never regaining consciousness. She died within the hour.

Did I want to face that tragedy? Yes. I

never blame God for tragedy or give him credit for accidents. I believe he gives us the freedom to do stupid things as well as honorable things in this great scheme of His. I could have escaped and avoided the unpleasantness of Mother's death. I could have stayed for only a moment, kissed the top of her head, and gone back to the lake to pick up the kid's. I could have been safely back in Grand Forks before she left this earth.

But I couldn't have done that because I would have never forgiven myself for missing the opportunity to be part of her death. I celebrated her life even as she lay dying. Her death gave me the opportunity to tell her one last time how much I loved her.

Father

Five and a half months after my mother's death, my father had a severe stroke. He couldn't speak for two and a half years. He was also took up residency in the nursing home in Hatton. The stroke, which robbed him of his speech and of his ability to prevent the saliva from running down his chin, did not prevent him from knowing what was going on around him. He enjoyed our Sunday outings to the farm and for the total love and support he received from his children. There is nothing I would not have done for my father. The memories of the drives we took to look at the fields during his confinement, are priceless to me. As we drove, he would point at things and I'd figure out what he was saying. Sometimes we would go to the barn that we'd fixed up and he would point to the corner. It is possible that he pointed there because there used to be a hole in that corner where he used to come down the steps from the haymow. Perhaps he was trying to tell me to be careful, but I was never really quite sure. It was one of the few things we "talked" about that I couldn't interpret fully. I still look at that corner and think of my father, and try to figure out the message that may still be hidden there.

My father continued to deteriorate physically. When my father was hospitalized for the last time, my sister, brother-in-law, older brother, and myself were together around his bedside. My youngest brother was not able to be there with us at the time because of the wedding of his daughter. We knew the end of my father's life was near and as we stood around his bed, my father took my brother-in-law's hand and said, "ouekjlkj bodkshbsh." Then Don let go of his hand and he took Duane's (my older brother's) hand and in his inability to speak gave another garbled message: "objlkljb oielkjgmlvhb jjummjm." Then he let go of Duane's hand. My sister was next, and with the hand that was not paralyzed, he pulled her to him in a firm embrace and as she stood again, he said," ogmjforklmglksjl golskjldgn klskdj."

Then it was my turn. He talked a long time in this same uninterpretable pattern. When he was through, I said, "Dad, I just don't know what you are saying, but I think it is something nice."

He smiled at me and continued because his mind was still thinking the words, but they weren't coming out as he thought them.

Later, my sister Shirley said to me, "Luther, you know what he was telling you don't you?"

"Yeah," I kind of grinned.
"He was thanking you," she said.

But it was me who was thankful. Thankful for the life that my mother and father had given me. Thankful to be able to spend their last years with them, their last days, their last moments. Death can sometimes be a blessing in disguise. It makes us focus on what is important in life.

My brother, brother-in-law, and sister then left to go to my niece's wedding. Joanna and I volunteered to stay with Dad. Within a short time, he slipped into a coma and died while I held his hand.

CHAPTER SEVEN

Home and Family

Children

I didn't get married until I was twenty-eight years old. Coincidentally, my marriage occurred shortly before one of the neighbors said to me, "We had talked about you. We worried about you." That could have meant a variety of things. Perhaps the neighbors were afraid that I had stayed on the farm too long and had missed my chance with all of the eligible females. Perhaps the neighbors were experiencing an unspoken fear that I had a preference for "Ole" instead of "Lena". Or, perhaps, they were afraid I would not have someone to slurp coffee with me during the traditional lunches sprinkled periodically throughout the day.

What a relief it must have been to them when I had the good fortune of finding a beautiful, sensitive wife with whom I have been able to share in the highs and lows of my life. And, as if that weren't enough, I was blessed with five children who we love. Five children conceived by every known method of birth control. Five children who have grown up to be people I am proud to have made contributions toward. (Some of those contributions were even in addition to gasoline, money, furniture and cars.)

And even though I am a Norwegian and my wife is a German, all five of our children are Norwegian. That is possible because a

Norwegian sperm doesn't need an egg for fertilization. It simply needs a place to rest.

I have to admit, though, that becoming a father was a little like learning to drive a car when the vehicle was already in gear and going down a steep incline at one hundred miles per hour. And, then, when reaching a sharp curve, finding the brakes are gone. So much happened so quickly. I became a husband, a father and a happy man all on the same day. I started out with a four year old daughter. The only parenting tools I came equipped with was the desire to instill the Golden Rule. Time proved that one tool to be a survival kit, and it was enough to carry me through the three more daughters and one son that were to follow.

One of the times I have truly appreciated the rewards bestowed on a parent, occurred this past Christmas. It perhaps isn't a gargantuan episode of parental bliss in everyone's eyes, but it was one of those moments we dream about when we are changing diapers or surviving the teen years.

On Christmas Eve we were opening gifts and I was settled into the recliner as I am inclined to do even on non-holidays. My son and his family were at our home along with our youngest daughter, Lucy. I had opened a gift from Lucy already, but I was handed an envelope from her also. I opened it and there was a check for $100.00. It was a return of some money I had lent her, and accompanying the check was a hand-written note that said, "I really appreciate your lending me this money. I won't guarantee that I won't be asking for money in the future. In fact, I am sure I will. But I want you to know how I feel. You are so important to me. Here are words that I hope will show you really how I feel." Then she wrote down the words to the popular song, "Wind Beneath my Wings".

I finished reading the note and looked up and saw Lucy looking at me from where she sat on the floor beneath the Christmas tree. I wiped the tears from my cheeks with the back of my hands and she came over, bent down, and wrapped her arms around me in a big hug. It was a special moment that will bring warmth to me each time I reflect on it in years to come.

Like all families we have had our struggles and have experienced distances between us. Most of these distances, however, have occurred when my children, knowing my standards and my values, have not adhered to those standards and values. Often times the distance is compounded by the fact that a child doesn't realize that it is a struggle for a parent also to strive for higher standards and goals, and the result is a respectful discomfort.

An example of discomfort occurred a few years ago. It wasn't a monumental experience, but one that is perhaps typical of homes across America when children come face to face with a conflict to their parents' values. It was a cozy, winter evening when my two youngest daughters were sitting in the family room with me and one of them said to the other, "Let's watch that Eddie Murphy movie."

"Yeah," I said, eagerly, anticipating a relaxing evening with two of my favorite people in the whole world.

"Let's watch it!" I boomed, "Put it in!" I settled into my easy chair, thinking about taking a break a little later to make popcorn; thinking about the memories I was making with my daughters; feeling life was good and thanking God for granting someone the technology to make a remote control.

The credits rolled; my precious daughters sat at my feet; the music reached a crescendo; and I sat, smiling, enjoying the role of "Dad" to the fullest. Then Eddie Murphy came on the screen with words that I have never used even when the car tire went flat on a country road in a rain storm - in the middle of a moon-less night.

I witnessed my two daughters looking uncomfortably at each other. They covertly sneaked glances toward me, then back to the television. For some unimaginable reason, Mr. Murphy's voice suddenly seemed to become louder and the words more disgusting. Before I could say anything about the situation, one of my daughters reached up and pressed the top button and took the movie out.

At that moment two thoughts passed simultaneously through my parental brain. First, there was a surge of pride that my daughters respected me enough to not submit me to something they felt compromised my standards; and secondly, the thought occurred that my standards aren't probably quite as high as they perceive them to be.

Through incidents like this, I have discovered that sometimes children neglect to see that parents are human beings also, with the same challenges, stupid and miserable thoughts, and selfish desires that their children have. Sometimes this knowledge makes us question our abilities to be role models. And sometimes, to complicate this delicate relationship between parents and children even more, our most famous role models have shattered the pedestal we place them on, too, and we, as adults, are unforgiving of it. (Remember when Jimmy Carter admitted to 'lusting in his heart'?) Is it no wonder that our children have difficulty understanding our weaknesses as parents, when we, as adults, sometimes criticize public people for stating publicly what we all do privately? If the truth were to be known, Jimmy has not been the only "good" person who has ever lusted in his heart. There were four or five others and rumor has it that one of them may even have been Scandinavian.

Joanna

A husband and wife is a complicated, yet simple and natural union. Like Ole said, "I love Lena so much I almost told her one time."

I think Joanna would agree that we have done everything we have wanted to do as husband and wife. I think she would even go so far as to say that when she asks me to do something for her, I ALWAYS do it. I tell myself, "Luther, don't be such a pushover. You don't have to do EVERYTHING you are asked to do." I get myself built up into this macho frenzy, ready to look her in the eye at her next request, and snarl, "Naw, won't do it. Got manly things to do right now."

But next thing I know, she'll be smiling sweetly and asking gently for some assistance or to go somewhere and suddenly, to comply with her request seems like the manly thing to do.

For the most part, our life together has been one long honeymoon. It hasn't all been perfect. We've hit some bumps along the way. I'm sure the time our future was unstable after I left the security of the University of North Dakota was difficult for Joanna. When we moved back to Hatton, Joanna went through a time that was difficult for me. But through it all, we have remembered how much we love each other.

An acquaintance of ours once commented to her husband, "Honey, we have been married for twenty-five years and you haven't told me love me since the day we were married."

Her husband replied, "I know. If I change my mind, I'll let you know."

As I have "matured" over the years, marriage has taught me how really very different men and women are, and how important it is that we examine these differences if we are going to live with each other for fifty years. I have gone to some fiftieth wedding anniversaries and I have not felt very good about the celebration because it appears that the couple has only existed together for that length of time. The relationship has not appeared to be wonderful and open and understanding. In fact they have just been together that long.

It reminds me of the Ole and Lena story where Ole walks downtown to the gas station on the day of his Fiftieth wedding anniversary. He is leaning dejectedly against a lamp post when Sven comes up to him.

"What's wrong, Ole?" Sven says.

"It is my fiftieth vedding anniversary, Sven," Ole replies.

"Ole, dat's wonderful! Dat is cause for celebration! Vy such a long face?" Sven asked.

"Well, Sven," Ole began. "Fifty years ago, I made a mistake and got Lena in da family vay. Her fadder held a gun ta me and said, 'Ole, you eidder marry Lena or go ta prison for fifty years.'

Then turning to Sven, Ole broke into a sob, "I vould have been a free man today!"

Many times in a marriage relationship I have heard someone say, "I thought I could change that person". That is a big mistake. Sometimes people think that if they love someone, they can do some changing. I have not seen any evidence in my lifetime that people make changes in each other through marriage. Instead, the results of attempting to change the other mate is often disastrous.

I am thankful everyday for the wonderful marriage I have. There will never be a perfect relationship between a man and a woman, nor between any two human beings, but a good marriage has the potential for a oneness that is near perfection. A good partner will make anyone have so much more potential. We will be many times more than we could be by ourselves when we find the right person to share our lives with. I know that I have been able to do many things I would not have been able to do if I had been alone. Marriage is thinking of the other person from the moment you get up in the morning. You have to love someone and know them pretty well in order to be able to do that.

CHAPTER EIGHT

Other Relationships

Friends

There is the old Scandinavian joke about the farmer who went to town after harvest. "Heard you had a bumper crop, Ole!" the hardware store owner said.

"Yeah," Ole replied, "but it took a lot out of the ground."

Sometimes Ole's type of negative attitude corrodes our relationships with other people. As I grow older, I find myself valuing more and more the people who eliminate the negative and concentrate on the positive in their relationships with others. They become good friends. When I think of a good friend's qualities I think first of "trust". A good friend is someone you can trust with your intimate secrets and who will know, without being told, that those words are not to go any further.

When someone shares some information with me, does that put a burden on me? The fact that person has shared with me, tells me there is some trust there and that person has some confidence that I will not misuse the information they have given me.

Some people think that they have to accompany information with the admonition: "Don't tell anybody." I always get a chuckle at this comment. Over the years the realization has struck that a person feeling the need to make this comment, has already told several people the same information. "Don't tell anybody!" usually simply means that they don't really trust your judgment or else they want to do all of the telling themselves.

Besides being trustworthy, a good friend is one who will not change the positive things you say into negatives with a little jealous twisting. They will support you at all times. Their value becomes more obvious as the years go by when proof of their friendship has been tested many times. I look back over the years and I see in my mind's eye the faces of many friends who are still just as pure and fresh and supportive as they were on the first day I met them. They are amongst my most valued treasures.

All of us experience temporary and false friends, especially if you are quite visible and people decide they want to go along for the ride. This "wanting to go along for the ride" happened literally when I was in the army. I had this beautiful black DeSoto. It had four doors. It was huge, almost limousine-like. The dealer I bought the car from neglected to tell me how to handle all the new friends that would come with it, most of whom didn't have a car.

I soon developed a test to see who really were my friends and who were the DeSoto's friends by saying, "If you want to ride with me to Savannah, Georgia, it will cost five dollars apiece." It worked. I had no trouble at all.

Another test for friendship is whether or not a person makes assumptions about you without ever getting to know you well, first. For example, if you drive a fancy car, people assume you are rich. If you are clean, dress well and your home is neat, they assume you are rich. If you are happy, people think you have money because they associate happiness with wealth.

I truly feel, however, that above the poverty level which is adequate food, clothing, and shelter, happiness is inversely proportionate to the more material things we have. The more material things we have, the more unhappy we are. Sociologists have come to this conclusion and I sincerely agree with it. There is never enough. It is part of the human condition to always want more. We have seen examples of the richest people in the world being very unhappy. The Royal Family in England is a perfect example.

Assumptions, therefore, can cause unjustified antagonism. When we moved out to Beaver Creek, because I had been on television, people thought we were rich. We cleaned up the farmstead, painted the buildings and really cleaned things up and people said things like, "What have you got, a money tree?" I heard it many times. I have to admit that those types of comments were painful for several reasons: The people saying them did not appreciate our efforts for what they were - a labor of love and pride, and they made assumptions that were unfounded and seemingly jealousy-induced.

It is amazing that our weaknesses are our strengths and our strengths are our weaknesses. For example a friend will think someone is "enthusiastic" and a foe will say "he talks too much". A friend will say "he's happy" and a foe will say, "he doesn't know when to take things seriously". "He's humble" vs. "He's very quiet and shy." We can go mad trying to please everyone. It is not possible. We can only try to be the best friend we can possibly be and not pass judgement on anyone else.

What's In a Name?

Sometimes, when the skies are dark and I haven't seen a good friend for what seems like a very long time, I'll hear a cherished voice say my name. It is odd, isn't it, how hearing our name, mellows us? There is no more powerful word than our names.

To hear my name when I was a teenager, especially if it was a girl who said, "Hi, Luther", instead of just "Hi". Ohhh I would just melt. When she would say my name, I thought it would lead to something long-term like marriage or something. I would think, "Boy, does she want to go out with me!" even though it probably meant nothing more than any other greeting she used.

Knowing the effect of a name on a person, is something I use when I speak now. If I am at a banquet and there is a social hour with name tags, I'll go around to various people, extend my hand, and after reading their name tag, I'll say, "Hi there, George!"

The usual response is, "You remember me!"

and they gush. I could sell them a car with no brakes. It doesn't matter at that point that I didn't ever know them, let alone remember them.

Another example of the importance of names was demonstrated at the university when we purchased a machine that allowed us to personalize the computerized form letters we sent out to perspective students. The impact of putting a name in a letter became obvious very quickly. After our first mailing in this new system, a young girl came up to me and said, "I am going to the University of North Dakota next year. I got this two page letter from Doctor Rowe in the business education department. It was addressed to me and signed by him. It was so nice." She even had the letter with her. I did not tell her it was done by machine. How she felt about it was much more important than the actual technology that gave the personal impression.

To be ignored is the worst thing. To be called by your name is one of the best things in the world.

The Importance of Communication in Family Relationships

If relationships amongst strangers, neighbors and friends is a delicate balance, then the relationship between family members is infinitely more delicate. The importance of continued communication is vital in preserving the wonderful institution of family. There will always be conflicts in family and working out the problems isn't always easy, but it is always worth the effort.

An example of a personal family conflict that comes to mind, is one that many families deal with; The problem of who gets to buy the family farm. I have two brothers and a sister and when my father offered to sell me the farm, I was careful to not offer more that its worth so that there would be no question of my out-bidding my brothers and sister. My older brother and sister had no interest in buying the farm and were surprised that I was interested. My younger brother, however, wanted part of the farm for sentimental reasons.

My younger brother is nine years younger than the rest of us and so had spent nine years on the farm by himself after the rest of us had grown up. We knew there was some sentimental attachment, but we also knew that he was not interested in farming and not, at the time of the selling, in a position to purchase the entire farm. What we didn't know was how truly interested he was in having a portion of the land until that summer day.

My dad came to Grand Forks to visit me one day and we were driving to the donut shop for coffee, just the two of us when he said out of a clear, blue sky, "Now they all want it."

"What?" I said.

My father tried to explain, as I drove along South Washington Avenue and I glanced toward him and saw tears streaming down his cheeks. Suddenly I lost my way. I lost my way to a coffee shop on a familiar street that I had been on thousands of times. I took a wrong turn, pulled over and parked the car. I had lost my direction, but the direction wasn't important any more.

Dad explained to me that the "they" and "all" he was talking about, really meant only my younger brother and his wife. We sat and talked about it for a while. "Dad, didn't you tell him that it is too late? The paper work is already done and it has been paid for?"

"No," my dad said. And I looked at his tormented face and realized that having just lost his companion of fifty-five years, left him with only his children and he did not want them to be divided. He just wanted everybody to be happy.

We proceeded to the donut shop and as we had coffee, I said, "I'll tell you what, Dad. If there's a problem, I'll tear up the contract. Do you want me to tear up the contract?"

"No!" he said, vehemently.

"Well, Dad, don't worry about this," I said. "I will call Darrell and we'll talk about it."

I called Darrell that night and said, "Darrell, I understand there is a problem here."

"I would like part of the farm," Darrell said.

"What would you do with it? Separate it? And there are four of us too, remember," I replied.

As we visited, I could tell that Darrell wasn't thinking of the farm from a business standpoint. He was emotionally tied to it, so I told him, "If you really feel that strongly about it Darrell, these things don't mean that much to me and I'll tear up the contract."

"No. No. " he said.

And so things were left as they had originally been. Oh, there were many discussions over the next few years. Words that stung a little, were spoken. Some confusions were cleared up. But we were never nasty to each other. Not once. We kept talking until we understood each other and where we were coming from. Then one day, some time later, my brother and his wife visited the farm and agreed that they would never have fixed up the buildings the way we had. Then I knew we had been on the right track all along.

Every human being on the face of this earth is an individual. We all have things about us that are different from one another. We are like snow flakes with no two individuals being alike. We can understand each other to a certain point, but the rest of the understanding must come through communication. We need to remain open to each other so that we can learn to understand, care and love each other.

Even at my age, I feel that I am just in the learning stage where the world and universe are concerned. I need input from others as to what is happening around us. I am in awe of the stars that take millions of years for their beam of light to hit us, and the realization that by the time that light gets to us, the star that produced it is perhaps already burned out.

How can we worry about petty arguments when we are going through space at a speed of 88,000 miles per hour and turning around at about 18,000 miles per hour - constantly expanding and moving? We insignificant human beings do not have the right nor the power to do anything but be grateful and open to other people and to nature around us.

CHAPTER NINE

Religion

Lefse is Manna

We are often told by even our churches that we are sinners; we fall short; we are not worthy. That was the attitude of the church I grew up in. What does that do to the self-concept of a child? In my case, there weren't life-long dire consequences because I had a mother who seemed to think I was alright, even if I sometimes walked the narrow, invisible line between heaven and hell. She loved me. And as long as you have a few people around you who really love you and allow you to become the person that you can be, not even people's misguided interpretation of God's word can mess you up.

When I became an adult, sometimes Mother and I would get into heated discussions about what was acceptable by God and what wasn't. It may be helpful to understand Mother's religious beliefs by knowing the circumstances in which she grew up. When she was a young child, her mother died and her father simply disappeared. Mother was raised by her grandmother. Everything she read was carefully censored and monitored. The result was an extraverted women raised in a somewhat stifling environment.

My mother's conflicted upbringing was evident in the discussions we would have about religion. We could discuss anything, and often times I would play the devil's advocate

ABOUT THE AUTHOR:

1st RECORD ALBUM

Widely known and widely traveled, Luther Bjerke has made his mark on the Upper Midwest as a speaker of uncommon distinction. Speaking to groups ranging from 50 to 5,000, he skillfully blends a style of comedy and insight. Entertaining and yet provocative, he brings a lighthearted, spritely and positive message to his audiences.

Luther Bjerke speaks as one who has worked with both the light and earnest sides of people for more than 20 years. A man of humble beginnings, he was born in the tiny Norwegian settlement of Beaver Creek and received his early education in a one-room school near Hatton. In later life he moved to the northeast (of Hatton, that is) and the great metropolitan area of Grand Forks where he enrolled as a student at the University of North Dakota. Upon graduation he worked briefly with the American Red Cross as a field representative in the Midwest. He then spent 15 years on the staff of UND talking to high school students and counseling new freshmen on their college careers.

In addition to his busy professional life, Luther has delighted thousands throughout the years, particularly with his portrayal of "The Wild Norwegian from Beaver Creek." His audiences have come home with memories of an enjoyable experience and something else — a message about the happiness and achievement that can be found within all of us.

Luther also holds two University degrees and has been:

- A University Associate Dean
- A University Director of High School Relations
- An Assistant Professor
- President of the United Fund and Campaign Director
- Chairman of Greater Grand Forks American Red Cross Chapter
- Elected to Who's Who in American Colleges and Universities
- The list could go on - but who cares

I GREW-UP LISTENING TO THIS RADIO

This L - Tatro Radio that Luther listened to for the first seventeen years of his life. A thirty-two volt wind powered generator provided the power for him to enjoy programs like; Jack Armstrong, The Green Hornet, Amos and Andy, Jack Benny, Abbot and Costello, Fibber McGee and Molly, Inner Sanctum, Hermits Tales and others.

2nd Record Album

On 17th of May

Luther Bjerke is glad his kids turned out Norwegian

By Marilyn Hagerty
Herald People Editor

HIS BLUE EYES light up. The Norwegian blood courses through his veins. And Luther Bjerke says, "I get excited about the 17th of May."

This is the day the Norwegians celebrate their Independence, and Bjerke — who is a full-time Norwegian — has seen it happen. Right there in Oslo.

A couple of years ago he was in Norway, and he says, "On Syttende Mai I watched King Olaf salute the people, and the parade went on for three hours."

When people around Grand Forks think of Norwegians, they usually think of Bjerke and his stories about Lena and Ole.

He started making a few casual speeches ten to 15 years ago about them and his old home at Beaver Creek, N.D.

Since then, he has gravitated to a full time occupation as a speaker. For the past year, this Norwegian who says funny things with a straight face has been doing very well, thank you.

He hops from Hampden to Neche and down to Fargo. Sometimes he is billed as the "Wild Norwegian."

More often of late, he is being called an inspirational speaker.

He has gone beyond Norwegian humor and mixes in his homespun philosophy As he travels the Red River Valley, Luther Bjerke talks about attitude.

"We are what we think we are," he says.

And his message is spreading wider and wider as he accepts invitations to places like Memphis, Minneapolis and Denver.

"I always start out with a little Norwegian humor," says the man from Beaver Creek.

Indeed he says, there is a Beaver Creek. "I was born there in 1930, and I made quite an impression on my mother. I weighed 11½ pounds when they put me on a scales two days later. There's shrinkage, you know. I might have weighed 14 pounds."

On careful questioning, Bjerke admits his mother isn't all that Norwegian. But his father, Elmer, a retired farmer, is 100 per cent Norske.

He says his wife, Joanna, isn't Norwegian, either. She's German. But Bjerke is sure glad his five children all turned out Norwegian.

As a boy, Bjerke says he was never shy. He loved to sing and speak pieces at Beaver Creek Lutheran Church. He skipped fourth grade at Beaver Creek 5 central school.

'In Oslo on Syttende Mai, King Olaf appears, and the parade lasts three hours'

And since his mother noticed he had a hard time being serious, she kept a supply of jokes and readings around the houses.

Bjerke admits it was difficult adjusting to seventh grade in Hatton.

He says he just figured since he was from Beaver Creek 5 he would have to try harder. When he finished high school in Hatton in 1947 at the age of 16, he stuck around the farm for four years. He took on various jobs including that as a water safety instructor for area camps.

"I was just gathering momentum," he says. "I needed that."

Bjerke has fun at everything. Even the army.

"I fought a peacetime war at Fort Huachuacu, Ariz.," he says. After that, he enrolled at the University of North Dakota. When he graduated in 1959, he went to Kansas as the youngest field representative the Red Cross ever hired.

Two years later, he came back to the University of North Dakota as a recruiter. By the time he struck out on his own last year he was associate dean of the University College.

Giving up a good salaried position to go into full-time speaking and Norwegian humor wasn't an easy decision.

But, Bjerke says, he knew he couldn't be happy in the mold he found himself in for the next 20 years. He reasons, "Security is a state of mind. If you sit around and wait, your life will be over before you do anything."

And now, a year later, he is finding he gets enough speaking engagements and "spin offs" to pay the mortgage on his home at 2804 Walnut St., cover the insurance on the cars and handle the grocery bills.

Bjerke has been paid as much as $700 for one speaking engagement, and he makes some talks for nothing.

"I do have a fee schedule depending on the organization and what I am asked to do," he says.

He has received as many as five invitations after one banquet. He has bookings as far ahead as April of 1978.

No one has ever chosen the route of full time humorist and speaker and succeeded in a rural area, but Bjerke seems to be doing it.

To do it, he keeps his material fresh.

He spends hours reading and preparing — but he never uses a manuscript.

That way, he says, each talk is spontaneous.

Bjerke says, "I have been called naive, but I think a little naivete is good. I eliminate the negative things in my life, and I am happy."

It all harks back, he supposes, to his days in Beaver Creek during the depression. "We didn't have all the things in the 1930s that people have now," he says. "Yet we laughed about things.

"I am finding happiness evades too many people today. We have forgotten to laugh, and we have to be reminded."

Luther Bjerke Mixes homey philosophy with Norwegian humor

Permission from Grand Forks Herald

Some Newspaper bits...

ATTITUDE

LUTHER BJERKE

NOTED
EDUCATOR,
HUMORIST, AND
INSPIRATIONAL SPEAKER

....................LOOKING GOOD?.........FEELING GOOD?.............

YOUR ATTITUDE MAKES ALL THE DIFFERENCE IN THE WORLD....A HEALTHY SELF IMAGE IS OF THE UTMOST IMPORTANCE TO YOUR MIND, YOUR HEALTH, AND YOUR GENERAL WELL BEING. COME AND HEAR LUTHER BJERKE, IT MAY ONLY CHANGE YOUR LIFE.

U. CENTER 8:00

Bjerke forsakes recruiting for public-speaking career

Wild Bjerke Laughs Up Brass Rail

Bjerke to speak

Luther Bjerke, Grand Forks, will be the main speaker at the annual convention of the North Dakota Lumber Dealers Association Friday at Fargo.

Commercial Club sets Ladies Night

Luther Bjerke, Grand Forks, will be the featured speaker at the North Dakota Sheriff's and Police Associations Annual Convention at Jamestown tonight.

Positive thinking keeps Luther Bjerke going

Bjerke releases album for the holidays

"Wild Norwegian" seen on Today Show

Luther Bjerke, well-known Grand Forks humorist, will be speaking at the Outstanding Young Farmer contest which will be held Sn Sunday through Tuesday at Bismarck. Bjerke will speak at a Monday luncheon. A total of 39 states will be represented. Representing Minnesota will be Jerry Kruger, Warren, Minn., farmer. The event is sponsored by the Jaycees.

Best Sellers

The Gospel According to Beaver Creek (Luther Bjerke) 6.95

EASTERN NORTH DAKOTA DISTRICT
of
The American Lutheran Church
1325 - 11th Street South
Box 207 Fargo, N. D. 58102

STEIGER TRACTOR INC.

MINN-DAK BRAND CANARY SEED
FROM THE HEART OF THE RED RIVER VALLEY

MINN-DAK GROWERS ASSOC
GROWERS AND PROCESSORS OF MINN-DAK BRAND CANARY
Oil Sunflower - Sunflower for Human Food & Bird Food - Field Peas - Wild Bird

Wild Rice Electric Cooperative INC.
MAHNOMEN, MINNESOTA 56557

M/C M/C
MOORHEAD AREA
Chamber Of Commerce
824 CENTER AVENUE P. O. BOX 719 (218) 236-6200 MOORHEAD, MINNESOTA 56560

US
UNITED SUPPLIERS, inc.
Box 538 • Eldora, Iowa 50627
515-858-2341

FBS Leasing
Federal Reserve Bank of Minneapolis
250 Marquette Avenue Minneapolis, Minnesota 55480

American Farm Bureau Service Company
225 TOUHY AVENUE • PARK RIDGE, ILLINOIS 60068 • AREA CODE 312 399-5700

SAFEMARK

National Association of Home Manufacturers
6521 ARLINGTON BOULEVARD • FALLS CHURCH, VIRGINIA 22042
JOHN R. KUPFERER, Executive

SUPER VALU
SUPER VALU STORES, INC.
BISMARCK DIVISION
BOX 5506, BISMARCK, NORTH DAKOTA 58502
TELEPHONE 222 5600 / AREA CODE 701

THE CHAMPAGNE MUSIC OF LAWRENCE WELK

November 27, 1974

Mr. Luther Bjerke
2804 Walnut
Grand Forks, N. Dak. 58201

Dear Mr. Bjerke:

When I heard you in Fargo I felt that perhaps some day you could come and do a Norwegian bit on our television show--about two or three minutes. I thought perhaps you could create a little talk or comedy bit about Myron Floren, the happy Norwegian, or myself, a German. Due to the fact that we both play accordion and are associated with music and polkas and we are both from the Dakotas--he's from South Dakota and I'm from North Dakota--you might create a little chatter about the two of us in your usual Norwegian style.

I must confess I thoroughly enjoyed your little talk you gave while I was home.

Another thought you might be able to get into your little speech--I recall many years ago North and South Dakota were both fighting about where Sitting Bull was to be buried. That might lend itself to a little comedy bit. Now this idea may not be any good and if you don't think it is you can ignore it but, if you think it would be fitting, it may be enjoyable especially for the Norwegian people in North Dakota.

After you finish your bit I would explain that you are a good friend of mine, how we met and how much I enjoyed you.

Do you think my thoughts have any possibilities? Along with my suggestions, you can think about it and come up with your own thoughts for a comedy routine.

With best wishes.

Sincerely,

Lawrence Welk

Lawrence Welk
LW:ll

On a visit to Escondido, California

just for the sake of discussion. Only twice, however, in all of the discussions we had, did I find Mother, during the full excitement of the discussion, look skyward and a glaze come over her eyes.

Those two times, I said, "What's the matter, have we gone too far?"

"Yup," she responded and the conversation ceased between us.

But the conversation never really ceased for me. Inside I carried it on, comparing what I had been taught as a child to what I had found out from observing and experiencing the world, reading the philosophers and psychologists, studying the Bible and examining other people's beliefs.

When I think of religion and spirituality, the hymn that contains the words, "built on a rock, the church must stand, all other ground is shifting sand", as telling us that we must each examine our beliefs and work hard to verify and strengthen them so that we are on a solid foundation.

We cannot have a full life without having a spiritual existence. I have full spirituality and am so satisfied and happy that I do not want man's dogmas to tear me down and interfere with my relationship with God.

Lutheran religion, to me, is one of the most free forms of religion on the face of the earth. We have very few "do's" and "don'ts" in comparison with all of the other religions. With that freedom we should be able to have a full life.

Christ came down to earth and said, "I came so that you may have a more abundant life." He didn't say, "I came so that you may have a more abundant life if you don't do this or that."

When people want you to believe exactly the way they do, there is a void in your life. I love the church and would miss it terribly if I couldn't go every Sunday. But I believe it is vitally important that every aspect of the church be examined in order to attain a full spirituality. We must be open to everything without being judgemental.

I sometimes do an exercise that I think represents the concept of God in terms that are easy to understand. Take a piece of paper and at the top right-hand corner write the word "God" and underline it. Then at the top left-hand corner, write the word "Devil" and underline it. Then draw a line between these two words down the center of the paper. Now in the two columns write words that are representative of the word at the top of the column. Under the word "Devil" you will see words like "evil", "negative", "cynical", etc. Under the word "God" you will inevitably write words like "good", "loving", "positive".

After making your list, which column would you choose for yourself? Would you choose to be part of the negative list? Or does the positive list seem more appealing? It is entirely up to each of us. We all have a choice and nobody makes it for you. We have the responsibility of our lives.

Ole and Sven had a responsibility for their lives too. Both of them died in tragic accidents and found themselves at the pearly gates talking with Saint Peter at the same time.

"What happened to you?" Saint Peter asked Sven.
"I froze to death," Sven replied.

"That's tragic," Saint Peter replied and then turned to Ole. "What happened to you, Ole?"

"I came home from vork von day and as I vas taking off my shoes, I noticed that der was shoes vare mine shud have been. Den it dawned on me, dat perhaps somebody had been vit my Lena, so I looked all tru da house, even checking in da basement. As I vas running back up da basement steps, I had a heart attack an' died."

Then Sven said, "Ole, if you'd just checked the freezer, ve vould both be alive today."

A sense of humor is one of God's greatest gifts, I believe. In fact, the pastor who eulogized entertainer, Bing Crosby at his funeral, rephrased one of the Beatitudes this way, "Blessed is he who makes people laugh, for the laughter he creates is music to the ears of God. "

****

Even Lutefisk is Biblical: It is a piece of "Cod" that passeth all understanding."

CHAPTER TEN

Experiences that Contribute to a Life

The Fiji Islands

Sometimes, in reflection, there are certain times and coincidences that come readily to mind, that have exemplified the pre-destination of my life. One of those coincidences took place right in my hometown of Hatton, North Dakota. One night on my way home from a speaking engagement, I stopped at a lounge in Hatton. There were only two people in the bar and it appeared that they had been there for a very long time.

As I walked in, one of the guys hollered, "Hi, Luther!" at the same time as one of my Brekke Travel advertisements for a trip to Hawaii came on the television overhead.

"Ah, Luther," the guy slurred, "I don't want to go to Hawaii. I want to go to the Fiji Islands."

"What did you say?" I asked. "Did you say you wanted to go to the Fiji Islands?"

He said, "Yeah!" and then proceeded to tell me about being in the war and going to the Fiji Islands for some rest and recuperation.

"Was that an army group?" I asked.

"Yeah. The 164th Infantry."

This became a challenge. The guy in the bar didn't even know the name of the commander for the 164th, even though he had attended the reunions for 35 of the forty years they were held. I found out that the group was meeting in Dickinson in early October and found out who the commander was and called him. I asked to meet with him. "Sure, come on out and we'll introduce you at an opportunity there."

When I got to the reunion, I was introduced during the social hour. I got up on the bandstand and announced that I was planning a trip to the Fiji Islands. Chris Brekke of Brekke Travel had done some calling for me to get some information from travel agents in the Fiji Islands, so I had a lot of information with me when I made the announcement. I asked that if anyone was interested in traveling there, to let me know.

We ended up going to the Fiji Islands for two weeks. There were thirty-eight people in the travel group and we had a great time. The Governor General of the Fiji Islands, it turned out, had been a scout with the 164th Infantry in World War II. He had been appointed by the Queen of England to his position. He regaled us with his tales of his great grandfather who had been a cannibal chief and how his grandfather's people had eaten missionaries and each other. He described the process of boiling the people before eating and how it was considered a religious experience.

We also had the great privilege of going to the palace where I introduced everyone in our traveling group as they came in through the palace doors, announcing where they were from and what their position had been in their unit. The Island also had a parade in the visitors' honor as well as a band concert and a church service. It was the most fabulous trip of my life, and it all developed from one short conversation between myself and a guy who'd had too much to drink. A conversation that could have easily been overlooked or quickly forgotten.

The only sad part of this story was the fact that the man in the bar at Hatton who would rather have gone to the Fiji Islands than to Hawaii, never got to go. He could not go with, he explained, even after I offered him financial assistance. He missed out on an opportunity of a lifetime.

When we got back, I got a call from the editor of the 164th newspaper. The editor said, "I see you are speaking at the Kirkwood (a hotel in Bismarck, ND). Could I meet you for breakfast? I'd like to interview you about the trip and how it came about."

I didn't have any idea what he was going to ask me. As far as I was concerned, the trip had just been a routine one as far as arrangements went. We had a group of people who had wanted to go somewhere, so we made the arrangements and went.

As the editor was interviewing me, he asked, "How did you tie this in with the committee?"

"What committee?" I asked.

The editor explained that a committee had

been working on a trip of this sort for a long time. "You mean you never worked on this trip with the committee assigned to arrange it?"

It appeared that Brekke Travel and I had arranged and executed a trip in a short time, that the committee of the 164th had been unable to organize over a very long period of time.

The editor looked a bit perplexed and then said, "I'll write this story and the interest that was shown all of these years, but I can't say that all of a sudden you come along without knowing all of this and do it anyway. So would you mind if I just tie it in with the fact that you MAY have worked with the committee? I'll leave it sort of open so that it looked like you followed up on the committee's action."

I looked the editor of the 164th tabloid in the eye and said, "I'm telling you something right now. That trip would have never come off if I had worked with this so-called committee."

And when the article came out, it just flowed right into this. Isn't that wonderful? Do not close yourself to opportunity. Often times people do a lot of talking and other people don't pay attention to it. Sometimes listening carefully pays off.

We need to take risks in our lives. A life without risk is not worth living. The greater the risk, the greater the commitment. A life with no problems is no life at all. Dr. Norman Vincent Peale was asked by a fellow one time, "Dr. Peale, you have done so much for people, and I am overwhelmed by my problems and my difficulties."

Dr. Peale told the man, "I can help you. I can take you to a place where people reside who have no problems at all."

The fellow said, "Take me there!"

Dr. Peale said, "I certainly can. It's the cemetery."

Positive Reinforcement

Another incident that contributed to my life occurred when I was on a plane flying to Chicago one day, and I found myself sitting by a gentleman from Pioneer Hybrid Seed Company. He was the same man who, a few years before, had hired me to speak on their company tour for three years in a row. This had been a special time in my life. It was big-time as far as I was concerned. They made all of the arrangements, paid me well, and even sent a person from the main office to accompany me on the circuit.

As we visited on the airplane, now, several years later, the fellow said to me, "You're still doing the same thing aren't you?"

I said, "yes."

"Wonderful. Don't ever change that. I'll tell you why. I've been listening to these preacher-type motivators and they sound like a canned version of what they are saying, and that if you interrupted them, they'd have to start over." Then he added, "Luther, don't ever change. When you give a talk it sounds as if it is coming right from your heart."

It was one of the finest compliments I have ever received.

Revisiting Home Grounds

Another incident that has had an influence on me in recent years, was a return to the school I attended as a youth, Hatton Public School, to speak to a group of students about my life as a speaker, writer, and singer. At a time in life, when I had begun to question whether or not what I had to say was still pertinent to young people, it was a rewarding experience.

As I sat in my old gymnasium and looked at the fresh, unwrinkled faces before me, memories of my own school days flooded my thoughts. The children sat all around my chair and their teachers, Mrs. Donalee Strand and Mrs. Plaine were sitting with them.

I began by telling the students how everybody in the room has a book or record album in them. I showed them my first book and my record albums and explained to them that even if they don't think they can do these same things, that it is important to remember that they can do whatever they want to do and that they don't have to do anything alone. I explained that we all need others to help us and that we never really do anything completely alone.

The students and teachers were a wonderful audience. I left with a cookie, a jar of jelly, and the feeling that something had been accomplished, but not being able to put my finger on what that accomplishment might be. As I was leaving, however, I told the children, "If any of you want a record album, I'd be glad to bring one to you. We don't try to sell record albums any more. Now we sell tapes, so if you want an album, you can do with it what you want." I made it clear that I was just giving it to them.

Mrs. Strand saw me the next day and said, "They all want one."

So I autographed more than a hundred records and brought them to the school the following day and delivered them to the students' classroom. That was the moment that I knew that I had some affect on the children. They were so appreciative of the records and they laughed and applauded when I sang the songs, "Nincompoop" and "Lutefisk" to them.

And downtown that following week, the parents of several of the children commented to me about how excited their children had been about the records, the songs and the visit. The experience reminded me that even though I was hesitant about going to the school because I didn't have anything to offer them, I found out that taking the risk was worth it. Giving what I had was enough for them. And what they gave me back was priceless. They gave me back confidence in our youth and a feeling of self-worth.

Kogudus

Kogudus is an Estonian world that means

"fellowship". It is also the name of an organization I have had the good fortune to be a part of . A few years ago, about twenty of our members went to the penitentiary in Bismarck, ND, where we ministered to the inmates. We each stayed at our same table for the entire two days. We heard the heartbreak and stories of murders, rapists, embezzlers and thieves.

Several of the stories I heard in those two days will stay with me for the rest of my life. One story was that of an educated man who sat across from me. He had been a teacher and a family man. He was also a cold-blooded murderer. He had shot his wife, his wife's lover, and his brother-in-law.

The man told me about how he couldn't remember shooting these three people. He knew that he did it and that after he was arrested, he was told how he did it. He said, "I did not know what I had done until they told me. I was not surprised though, because I knew it was coming. There was something within me that was just going to explode and there was nobody I could talk to. Nobody I could share this with that I felt could handle what I was going through. I knew this affair was going on and all of a sudden, I just lost it and shot them. I have two daughters and now I found out that my sixteen year old daughter is pregnant and I cannot be with her."

It was at this point he broke down and cried before he was able to continue.

" That is the tragedy of being here," he said. "I can't be there at a time when she really needs me. I'm here until I die. I can't remember what I did, but I know I did it."

As a listener and a participant in fellowship with another human being, can I be judgemental of this man? No, I can learn from him as he gives me insight into what it is like to be a killer. A cold-blooded murderer. I cannot pronounce a judgement on him. That is God's business. My business was to help him find God and the peace He has to offer all sinners. My job is also to learn from the mistakes of this man and perhaps to share what I have learned with others.

CHAPTER ELEVEN

A Tying Together

You can't be happy unless you act happy. You can't be sad unless you act sad. One of the things I do when I speak to groups is to talk about appreciation. I tell the story about the wife who said to her husband, "Will you buy flowers for my funeral?"

The husband innocently answers, "Of course, sweetheart. I'll buy you a lot of flowers for your funeral."

"Well, sweetheart, instead of waiting until I die, why don't you buy them now?" the wife asks.

Then I tell the audience, "Before I go any further, reach out your hands to as many people as possible and tell them that you love them."

As I look out over the audience, I see a very few people hugging. I hear some people saying, "I like you." I see some people shaking hands and a few saying, "I love you."

Then I say, "Didn't that make you feel good, even if you didn't mean it? Of course some of you meant it. But here's the point: Don't think about it. The very act of reaching out and saying the words, helps to create the fact. If you make the effort to tell someone you love them, you will find yourself actually feeling that way after it is said."

The ability to lighten up is so important and crucial to a satisfying life. That is the purpose of this book. To help people to keep from growing old - too late smart. We should fill our lives with moments of excitement like those we experienced on Christmas Eve when we were children.

Remember that feeling? We didn't get such wonderful gifts to speak of as children. We'd get things like hand-me-down clamp skates. (You know, those skates that clamp to the bottom of your shoes that never really worked.) But it didn't matter. We'd go into skating with all the excitement necessary to have fun. Sure the skate would fall off with each movement, but that wasn't the point. The point was the excitement and anticipation.

The cows were never really milked dry on Christmas Eve. We'd go out and make feeble attempts at milking our eight cows while my sister and mother did the dishes. Then we'd come in and we were ready for the reading of the Christmas story and the opening of the presents. The anticipation and excitement was nearly overwhelming. We gloried in it. Everything anyone said was somehow sweeter or funnier than on any other day of the year. The food tasted better. The lights seemed to take on an ethereal glow. The paper on our packages were more colorful than colors can actually be. The air was filled with sugar and warmth, and a honeydew sweetness that one craves to capture in order to bring it out at will.

How sad that we feel that we get too old

to be excited.

Another sad commentary on some lives is our inability to take control of our own lives and to make good decisions for ourselves. President Eisenhower gave a talk to a group of high school senior girls, many years ago, and it was broadcast on a radio program I heard one time. The interviewer, after the speech, asked the President, "What is the most important advice you can give to these girls?"

Without hesitation, President Eisenhower said, "My most important advice is to learn to make decisions. If you make a wrong one, you can always change it."

I pondered those words at length. President Eisenhower was right. Without decisions being made, nothing happens. It is better for something to happen, even if it is not what was expected, than to have nothing happen at all.

Besides holding on to excitement and being able to make decisions, we must maintain, or even in some cases, develop a sense of humor. If you can laugh, you are in control of even those things that seem out of control. Why, even God has a sense of humor. Look in the mirror and see what he has created!

I was asked once, if it was true that some Scandinavians were buried with their head sticking out of the ground. and I asked, "Why in the world would they do that?"

The fella answered, "Because they last longer than tombstones.

A sense of humor can open lines of communication that haven't even existed before, because it relaxes the people around you. I remember a college professor who came into class once and said, "I was going to come into class on all fours this morning because my wife treats me like a dog, anyway." And I loved him right away. Humor is the essence of life - one of God's greatest gifts to us.

If a sense of humor is not one of your gifts, find what your gift is and develop it to its fullest potential. I don't care if you are eight years old or eighty years old. Discover what you like to do, what you are good at and then pursue perfection in it as quickly as you can. By perfection, I don't mean that every aspect of your gift will be flawless. That is not possible. What I mean is that you need to bring it to the fullest potential possible for you. The satisfaction that accompanies that fullest potential will be indescribably wonderful for you. Pursue your gifts now so that you can enjoy them for as long as possible.

Another word of advice I would like to offer, is to develop your mind constantly. You can transform your life by renewing and changing your mind. The only thing any of us have control of is our mind. Our body is a traitor as we age, but normally we can stay mentally alert and growing well into our old age. Our bodies are meant to carry our lives around. Our lives are really centered in our mind. Take care of your life. Make it grow even after your body stops. Make it be what you want it to be, even though your body may develop a form of its own.

Knowledge is life. I spent many years not being serious about the world around me - not bothering with any information that would cause me to stop and take stock of the magnitude of the world around me. I was totally carefree, but I did not know that I had not yet learned to live.

I learned to live once I realized that there was so much I wanted to know. Needed to know. I began reading self-improvement books. I began to listen to classical music along with my other music interests. I began to fill my empty vessel - a vessel that will never be full of knowledge no matter how long I live.

Our brain is like a muscle, basically. If you do not use it - you lose it. Do not hold back. Let yourself learn and grow. I have some friends who have stifled themselves so much from learning new things, that when they die their epitaph will say, "He was born. He had some coffee. And he died."

Our minds are like gardens which have seeds planted in them. Some of the seeds will grow into mature, life-giving plants. Some of the seeds may be those blown in by the wind from weeds. We must tend our garden, cultivating that which we wish to keep and plucking those plants that will choke out the good. We cannot put the gardens of our mind into summerfallow. We have no space for rotation. We must care for the only garden space we have.

Another important life-enhancing pearl to

keep in mind, is that we must surround ourselves with positive people. Stay away from complainers and negative people. They are more contagious and common than the common cold. Protect your mental health by surrounding yourself with people who look on the bright side of things. People who find the good in others and in each situation will help you find the good in your friends and situations, also.

Andrew Carnegie once commissioned an author by the name of Napoleon Hill to go out and talk to all of the successful people in the world and find out what made them tick. And Hill did just that. The constant he found in the lives of successful people was that they surrounded themselves with positive people, and if one negative person was found in their midst, they were ousted. None of these rich and successful people looked any different than anybody else. Their only difference was in their positive attitude and in the positive attitude in the people around them.

At the turn of the century, the book, Acres of Diamonds was written. It is a very special inspirational book about starting where you are in life. The story was about a man who had an obsession to find diamonds. He sold his farm to fund his search for diamonds, and ended up a broken man. He became broken of spirit and body, all without ever finding the diamonds he coveted.

The man, however, who had bought the farm from the broken man, was out working the fields one day, when he noticed shiny objects in the dirt. Beneath the broken man's very feet, had been acres and acres of diamonds.

The lesson is, of course, that we must be careful not to overlook what we already have. My acres of diamonds was Beaver Creek. I feel blessed to have been able to use my growing up years and love of speaking to become the only full-time professional speaker in the history of North Dakota. I want everyone to find their acres of diamonds and use their gifts to make the world a better place.

CHAPTER TWELVE

A Philosophy and a Purpose

Billy Graham, the famous evangelist, was being interviewed by Diane Sawyer on television one evening. During the interview, he discussed his fight with Parkinson's disease and how the symptoms seem nearly non-existent once he reaches the podium to preach the gospel. But I was totally surprised at the Reverend Graham's remarks when he was asked about who he thought he had influenced the most in his years of preaching. His response went something like this:

"I don't know if I have had an influence on anybody. I haven't done any great things. I feel that I am a failure because I have not accomplished one thing."

Isn't that something? One of the greatest evangelists of our time, feeling as if he hadn't accomplished anything because the condition of the world had not improved since he started preaching and he felt responsible for it. Then he was asked, "What do you want said about you and by whom?"

His response was: "I hope it is said about me that I did a good job and I want the Lord to say it. But I don't know if I will ever hear him say it."

These are words spoken by an evangelist that I respect more than any other evangelist because he preaches the gospel. And he isn't sure that he has done enough. It should make all of us examine our lives more closely.

If you should ask me if I feel that I have had on influence on people in my life time and if I felt I have done some good things, I would answer, "Yes!" I have felt that I really have the ability and have used it correctly, to help people laugh. If I could choose my epitaph it would be," He helped people laugh." He didn't make people laugh. He didn't laugh for people. He helped people laugh.

I am now at a point in life that I consider myself to be a bit of a philosopher. So in these mature years, if I can just use my knowledge accumulated over a life time to help others through times that may not be so easy for them, that would be the greatest gift that I could ever give myself. It would be the greatest gift I could ever give to others. Instead of dying, I want to be alive enough to help others, whether it is through laughter, teaching Sunday School or being president of the congregation.

Life was never meant to be simple. Life was never meant to be fair. But it WAS meant to be lived. Others can influence us in this process of living, but it is up to every individual to live whatever life that individual wants. There are certain guidelines, of course. My guidelines are that if it doesn't hurt myself, or others, or God, we can choose to do anything we want. They are simple guidelines, but perhaps guidelines that would be beneficial for everyone to follow. Within those guidelines, it is up to us to live either positively or negatively. It doesn't matter what happens to us in life. What really matters is how we feel about it and how we react to what has happened.

Take a few moments and think about your abilities and talents. Perhaps there are areas of interests and experiences that you have not even explored. Are you going to sit at some menial job that you hate what you are doing for the rest of your life because you like the salary? Or are you going to take some risks, try some things you have always wanted to do, be the best of whatever you are?

That simple decision to take control of your life and explore your talents can make the difference between saying, "I had a wonderful life. I did everything I wanted to do" or finding yourself in a nursing home, sitting in a wheel chair lamenting, "I should've done it den. It's toooo late now. I have ta sit here in dis chair. I can't do it now. I could have done it you know. But Uffda. But you know I could have done it."

We do better than we know how. We are guided by unseen hands when we are willing to go forward. The same road is not for all of us, even though the path may seem easier and wider when it has been traveled much. Like the poet, Robert Frost said, " Two roads diverged in a wood and I- I took the one less traveled by, and that has made all the difference." How profound.

Sometimes taking the road less traveled by as children labels us as stinkers. Perhaps some "stinkers" are really testing different roads, exploring their talents, measuring the risks while they still have parents that love them and can pull them back when the risk becomes too great. Sometimes "stinkers" are simply "thinkers" who do not yet have the experiences nor the vocabulary to share the importance of taking the road less traveled by, nor have the maturity of understanding how that can make all of the difference.

TEAR OUT THIS PAGE

Stinker to Thinker

By Luther Bjerke

Please send me _______ of your books, for which I enclose a check or money order for $ __________ . Cost is $9.95 each plus $2.50 postage and handling.

SEND TO:

Name ______________________________

Street Address ______________________________

City, State ______________________________

Zip ______________________________

BEAVER CREEK PUBLISHING

Route 2, Box 139A
Hatton, North Dakota 58240